Teacher's resource

150

Literacy Hour

Lessons

YEAR
3

Acknowledgements

The author and publisher would like to thank the following for permission to reproduce material in this book:

'Bet You Can't' © 1987 Penny Dale. Reproduced by permission of the publisher Walker Books Ltd., London. 'Lost!' by David McPhail reproduced by permission of the publisher LittleBrown, New York. 'Doctor de Soto' by William Steig reproduced by permission of the publisher Andersen Press Limited, London. 'Minibeasts' by Angela Royston published by Dorling Kindersley Ltd. © Dorling Kindersley Ltd., London. 'Summer' by Ruth Thomson reproduced by permission of the publisher Franklin Watts, London. 'Whatever Next!' by Jill Murphy reproduced by permission of the publisher Macmillan, London. 'Billy McBone' by Allan Ahlberg (from 'Heard it in the Playground'), 'I am Jojo' by Michael Rosen (from 'You Can't Catch Me!'), 'Fashion' by Brian Patten (from 'Gargling with Jelly'), 'Jim and the Beanstalk' by Raymond Briggs and 'Knock Knock Who's There?' by Anthony Browne reproduced by permission of the publisher Penguin Books. 'Mr Rabbit and the Lovely Present' by Charlotte Zolotow. 'The Great Blueness and other Predicaments' by Arnold Lobel and 'New Shoes' by Ffrida Wolfe (from 'Tiny Tim') reproduced by permission of the publisher HarperCollins, London. 'The Cheetah' by George Barker (from 'Runes and Rhymes and Tunes and Chimes') reproduced by permission of the publisher Faber & Faber, London. 'A New Coat for Anna' by Harriet Ziefert reproduced by permission of the publisher Random House Inc., New York.

Every effort has been made to trace and acknowledge ownership of copyright material but if any have been inadvertently overlooked, the publisher will be pleased to make the necessary alterations at the first opportunity.

First published 2001
exclusively for WHSmith by

Hodder & Stoughton Educational,
a division of Hodder Headline Ltd.
338 Euston Road
London NW1 3BH

Text and illustrations © Hodder & Stoughton Educational 2001

A CIP record for this book is available from the British
Library.

Author: Chris Lutrario
Series editor: Gill Matthews

ISBN 0340 78998 0

Typeset by Fakenham Photosetting
Printed and bound in Spain by Graphycems

Each term is divided into ten weekly themes, organised as follows:

• Objectives for the week
These are taken from the National Literacy Strategy Framework for teaching and form the basis of medium term planning for text, word and sentence level work.

• Resources
A list of the materials that are needed to teach the theme. Some themes are generic and a range of texts could be used while others are written around suggested texts.

Where necessary, preparation that can be carried out in advance is highlighted.

• Assessment
This is an outline of broad assessment objectives, recognising that many teachers already have detailed recording and assessment procedures in place in their schools.

• Lesson outlines
Each lesson is divided into the following sections:

Whole class
This section contains suggestions for whole class shared reading or writing activities. The final outcome of most themes is a completed piece of written work. The whole class teaching aims to guide children through the objectives in order to achieve this.

Group and independent work
This section contains ideas for group work, whether guided by you or another adult, or independent work. The suggested activity may be the task that you focus on with a group. How these activities are used will depend on your particular organisation.

Differentiation
Most lessons are accompanied by differentiated activities for high and low attainers and suggestions for where it would be suitable for children to work in mixed ability pairs.

Whole class
The final section of each lesson gives ideas for a plenary session, including:
- activities which revisit key learning objectives;
- feedback from children, either individuals, pairs or in some cases the whole class, on the work they have been doing;
- feedback from children on a partner's work;
- preparation for the next day's lesson
- class evaluation of a lesson or a theme of work.

• Photocopiable masters (copymasters)
Most themes are accompanied by photocopiable masters for use in whole class and group time. These are not work sheets to practise taught skills, but are closely linked to the content of the lesson. Many can be used as frames for collecting discussed ideas or for shared writing in whole class sessions, as well as by the children in group or independent work.

• Homework
Each theme is accompanied by a photocopiable homework sheet which explains to parents or guardians what the children have been doing in literacy work for that particular week. This is followed by a task that can be carried out by the child.

Throughout the themes the development of reading and writing skills are linked closely. Themes or blocks of themes start with an emphasis on the teaching of reading through shared reading, use the reading as a stimulus or model for shared writing and suggest ideas for children's writing based on the shared work that has been carried out.

Shared reading

The different reading organisations covered include:
- teacher reading to the children;
- children reading with the teacher;
- class reading without the teacher joining in;
- a group reading to the rest of the class;
- individual children reading to the class.

Shared writing

This book suggests activities whereby teachers model writing, provide a scaffold to support children in their writing and teach writing over a sequence of lessons. Children's writing should be used in shared sessions as a means of encouraging the early stages of drafting and improving writing.

Word level work

In order to ensure the appropriate emphasis and

How to use this book

focus it is often better to introduce word level work separately from text level work. Teachers will lead children in using their word level skills within shared reading and writing.

• Phonics

Phonic work should be used to support reading and children should be encouraged to see links between phonic activities, and shared and guided reading activities. Phonic work should also be incorporated into shared writing activities. Children can be encouraged to use word lists generated in phonic work to help with spellings. Many children find a class-made 'long vowel' dictionary a useful writing support.

• Word recognition, graphic knowledge and spelling

Word walls, lists and cards are ways of displaying and drawing children's attention to words that need to become part of their sight vocabulary. Recognition and practice of these words can be incorporated into shared and guided work.

• Handwriting

Most schools have adopted a particular handwriting scheme and many teachers have taken the practising of handwriting out of the Literacy Hour. However, modelled and shared writing provide good opportunities to demonstrate handwriting.

Teaching and learning strategies

A range of teaching techniques are suggested to make lessons interactive and ensure the involvement of all children. These include:

- Use of the 'time out' strategy during whole class sessions where pairs or small groups of children are given short periods of time to discuss a question, think of an appropriate word or compose a sentence.
- Pairing children during group work to encourage discussion and develop collaborative skills.
- Feedback from the class when sitting in a circle.
- Use of small whiteboards. These can be purchased from suppliers or made by laminating card and used with appropriate pens.
- Many teachers now make use of large white boards for shared writing and related activities. Large sheets of sugar paper may be more appropriate for some activities as they can be:
  - displayed as a model for writing;
  - used as part of a 'work in progress' display;
  - referred to as a memory jogger;
  - re-read as a familiar text, which can be particularly useful for low attaining children.

Speaking and listening

A range of suggestions for the inclusion of speaking and listening are included such as:

- organising a range of audiences for reading and for the sharing of written work;
- encouraging children to listen to each other in discussion about aspects of texts;
- asking children to respond to a range of questions, to give opinions and share ideas;
- making use of drama techniques such as 'hotseating', where some children are encouraged to take on a role and others to ask questions, during whole class work.

ICT

The amount of use made of ICT depends on many factors such as the hardware available and teachers' confidence in using it. A range of suggestions for its use are offered.

Word processing
The majority of writing activities that are carried out with paper and pencil can be fulfilled using a word processing package. Children's lack of word processing skills often makes tasks such as producing a final copy of a piece of written work laborious and time consuming. However, opportunities for word processing can be organised through tasks such as creating captions, labels, book titles and headings.

The Internet
The Internet may be used to find information relating to fiction and non-fiction work.

E-mail
There are a growing number of local, national and international projects making use of the school e-mail address to develop links with other groups and share information and ideas.

Word and sentence level activities
There are a growing number of programs available to support spelling development and the learning of certain grammatical structures.

Autumn term

	Theme	Objectives: children will be taught to:
1	Dialogue	Understand how dialogue is presented in stories. Be aware of the different voices in stories. Use reading as a model to write their own passages of dialogue. Begin to use paragraphing in presentation of dialogue in stories. Secure knowledge of question and exclamation marks. Recognise the basic conventions of speech punctuation. Use the term 'speech marks'. Notice and investigate a range of other devices for presenting texts, e.g. speech bubbles. Recognise a common vocabulary for introducing and concluding dialogue.
2	Fiction and non-fiction	Understand the distinction between fiction and non-fiction. Notice differences in the style and structure of fiction and non-fiction writing. Locate information using contents, headings and sub-headings. Make a simple record of information. Use awareness of grammar and other strategies in reading. Notice and investigate a range of other devices for presenting texts. Use independent spelling strategies. Collect new words from reading. Infer the meaning of unknown words from context.
3	Non-chronological reports	Notice differences in the style and structure of fiction and non-fiction writing. Locate information using headings and sub-headings. Read information passages and identify main points. Write simple non-chronological reports from known information. Identify boundaries between sentences in reading and writing. Write in complete sentences. Demarcate the end of a sentence with a full stop and start a new one with a capital letter. Recognise and spell common prefixes. Use knowledge of prefixes to generate new words from root words, especially antonyms. Use the term 'prefix'.
4	Organisation and presentation of information	Notice differences in the style and structure of fiction and non-fiction writing. Locate information using contents, index and headings. Compare the ways information is presented. Make a simple record of information. Notice and investigate a range of ways of presenting texts. Collect new words from reading. Infer the meaning of unknown words from context.
5	Playscripts	Read, prepare and present playscripts. Recognise the key differences between prose and playscript. Write simple playscripts based on their own reading and oral work. Take account of grammar and punctuation when reading aloud. Secure their knowledge of question and exclamation marks in reading and use in their own writing. Notice and investigate a range of other devices for presenting texts.
6	Poems of observation and the senses	Read aloud and recite poems. comparing different views of the same subject. Discuss choice of words and phrases. Distinguish between rhyming and non-rhyming poetry and comment on impact of the layout. Express views about a poem. Collect words and phrases to write poems. Design simple patterns with words. Recognise the function of verbs in sentences. Identify, blend and segment phonemes. Generate synonyms.
7	Story settings	Compare a range of story settings. Generate ideas relevant to a topic. Develop the use of settings in their own stories. Begin to organise stories into paragraphs. Practise new spellings. Collect new words from reading. Generate synonyms for high frequency words. Use the term 'synonym'.
8	Shape poems	Express views about a poem. Generate ideas relevant to a topic. Collect suitable words and phrases to write poems. Design simple patterns with words. Invent calligrams and a range of shape poems. Understand how the spelling of verbs alters when ing is added. Generate synonyms. Recognise common vocabulary for introducing and concluding dialogue.
9	Synonyms and thesauruses	Generate words relevant to a topic. Investigate the function of verbs in sentences through experimenting with changing verbs. Use independent spelling strategies. Practise new spellings. Understand the purpose and organisation of the thesaurus and use it to find synonyms. Generate synonyms for high frequency words. Use the term 'synonym'.
10	Verbs	Use awareness of grammar to decipher new or unfamiliar words. Investigate the function of verbs in sentences. Use verb tenses with increasing accuracy. Use past tense consistently for narration. Use the term 'verb'. Understand how the spelling of verbs alters when ing is added. Investigate and learn to use the spelling pattern le. Generate synonyms for high frequency words. Recognise common vocabulary for introducing and concluding dialogue.

Summary of objectives

Spring term

	Theme	Objectives: children will be taught to:
1	Characters	Identify and discuss main and recurring characters and evaluate their behaviour. Plan main points as a structure for story writing. Write portraits of characters. Investigate the function of adjectives in sentences (identify, collect and classify). Use the term 'adjective'. Understand the use of capitilisation for names. Recognise and spell common suffixes. Use knowledge of suffixes to generate new words. Use the apostrophe to spell shortened forms of words. Use the term 'suffix'.
2	Dictionaries	Identify misspelt words. Use independent spelling strategies. Investigate, spell and read words with silent letters. Recognise and spell words ending in common suffixes. Infer the meaning of unknown words from context. Use dictionaries to learn or check the spellings and definitions of words. Write their own definitions of words, developing precision and accuracy. Use the term 'definition'. Know the quartiles of the dictionary. Organise words alphabetically, using the first two letters.
3	Fables	Investigate the styles and voices of traditional story language. Identify story themes. Identify and discuss main and recurring characters. Plan main points as a structure for story writing. Describe and sequence key incidents in a variety of ways. Write a story plan for their own fable. Investigate the function of adjectives within sentences. Use the term 'adjective' appropriately. Understand how words change when *er, est* and *y* are added. Recognise and spell common suffixes. Explore opposites.
4	Making notes	Describe and sequence key incidents. Make clear notes, discussing and identifying purposes, identifying key words, exploring ways of writing in shorthand form, making use of simple formats to capture key points. Experiment with deleting words in sentences.
5	Myths and legends	Investigate the styles and voices of traditional story language. Identify story themes. Describe and sequence key incidents in a variety of ways. Write a story plan for a myth. Recognise the function of adjectives in sentences. Use the term 'adjective'. Experiment with deleting words. Practise new spellings. Understand how words change when *y* is added. Collect new words from reading. Infer the meaning of unknown words from context.
6	Performance Poetry	Choose and prepare poems for performance. Rehearse and improve performance, taking note of punctuation. Write new or extended verses for performance based on models of performance poetry read. Note where commas occur in reading, and discuss their function in helping the reader. Use the term 'comma' in relation to reading. Revise spelling of words containing long vowel phonemes. Discriminate syllables in reading. Use independent spelling strategies: sounding out and spelling phonemes.
7	Pluralisation	Extend knowledge and understanding of pluralisation. Use the terms 'singular' and 'plural' 'appropriately'. Understand the differences between verbs in the first, second and third persons. Practise new spellings. Investigate and identify basic rules for changing the spelling of nouns when s is added. Use the terms 'singular' and 'plural' appropriately.
8	Traditional Stories	Investigate the styles and voices of traditional stories. Identify typical story themes. Identify and discuss main and recurring characters. Write a story plan for own traditional tale. Write sequels to traditional stories. Recognise the function of adjectives within sentences; experiment with deleting and substituting; collect and classify. Recognise other uses of capitalization. Recognise and spell common suffixes.
9	Reading Instructions	Identify the different purposes of instructional texts. Discuss the merits and limitations of instructional texts to give an overall evaluation. Recognise how written instructions are organised. Read and follow simple instructions. Note where commas occur in reading and discuss their functions in helping the reader. Use the term 'comma'. Recognise and generate compound words. Explore opposites.
10	Writing instructions	Write instructions. Extend knowledge and understanding of pluralisation. Use the terms 'singular' and 'plural'. Note where commas occur. Identify misspelt words. Use independent spelling strategies. Identify and use basic rules for changing the spelling of nouns when s is added.

Summer term

	Theme	Objectives: children will be taught to:
1	Alphabetical texts and indexes	Scan indexes etc. to locate information. Locate books by classification in class or school libraries. Use IT to bring to a published form. Make alphabetically ordered texts. Understand how sentences can be joined in more complex ways. Use independent spelling strategies: sounding out and spelling using phonemes; by analogy. Collect new words.
2	Book reviews	Refer to significant aspects of the text. Compare and contrast works by the same author. Be aware of authors; discuss preferences and reasons for them. Write book reviews. Summarise orally the content of a text. Write letters (to authors about books). Revise and extend work on note-making from previous term. Summarise in writing the contents of a passage. Understand how sentences can be joined in more complex ways. Become aware of the use of commas in marking grammatical boundaries within sentences. Revise from previous terms: writing in complete sentences and sentence demarcation.
3	Characters	Refer to significant aspects of the text. Discuss a character's feelings, behaviour and relationships, referring to the text. Write openings to stories linked to reading. Write a first person account. Identify pronouns and understand their function. Use speech marks and other dialogue punctuation. Use the apostrophe to spell shortened forms. Collect synonyms which will be useful in writing dialogue.
4	Dictionaries	Scan alphabetical texts to locate information quickly and accurately. Use IT to bring work to a published form. Make alphabetically organised texts. Identify words within words. Recognise and spell prefixes *mis, non, ex, co, anti*. Use knowledge of prefixes to generate new words from root words. Explore homonyms. Understand that some dictionaries provide further information about words.
5	Extended story	Refer to significant aspects of the text. Discuss a character's feelings, behaviour and relationships. Plot a sequence of episodes as a plan for writing. Write more extended stories, set out in chapters and organised in paragraphs. Use speech marks and other dialogue punctuation. Recognise how sentences can be joined in more complex ways. Investigate how words and phrases signal time.
6	First and third person narratives	Refer to significant aspects of the text. Distinguish between first and third person accounts. Consider credibility of events in stories. Write openings to stories linked to reading. Write a first person account. Identify pronouns and understand their function. Ensure grammatical agreement. Use the apostrophe to spell shortened forms.
7	Humorous poetry and language play	Refer to significant aspects of a text. Compare forms or types of humour. Select, prepare, read aloud and recite poetry that plays with language or entertains. Use awareness of grammar to decipher new or unfamiliar words. Identify short words within longer words. Collect new words from reading. Explore homonyms.
8	Letters	Write a first person account. Read letters written for a range of purposes and audiences. Write letters, notes, messages. Experiment with recounting the same event in a variety of ways. Organise letters in simple paragraphs. Identify pronouns and understand their functions. Ensure grammatical agreement in writing of pronouns and verbs. Recognise how sentences can be joined in more complex ways. Collect, investigate and classify common expressions.
9	Poetry that uses sound	Refer to significant aspects of the text. Recognise rhyme, alliteration and other patterns of sound. Write poetry that uses sound to create effect. Revise spelling of words with long vowel phonemes. Identify, blend and segment phonemes.. Use independent spelling strategies: sounding out and spelling using phonemes; spelling by analogy..
10	Author study	Retell, compare and evaluate stories. Refer to significant aspects of the text. Compare and contrast works by the same author. Be aware of authors and discuss preferences. Plot a sequence of episodes as a plan for writing. Write openings linked to reading. Write book reviews for a specified audience. Understand how sentences can be linked in more sophisticated ways. Investigate how words and phrases signal time. Practise new spellings. Collect new words from reading.

Theme 1) Dialogue

Objectives

Text level:
- 2 understand how dialogue is presented in stories
- 3 be aware of the different voices in stories
- 10 use reading as a model to write own passages of dialogue
- 15 begin to use paragraphing in presentation of dialogue in stories

Sentence level:
- 6 secure knowledge of question marks and exclamation marks
- 7 recognise the basic conventions of speech punctuation
- 8 use the term 'speech marks'
- 9 notice and investigate a range of other devices for presenting texts – *speech bubbles*

Word level:
- 19 recognise a common vocabulary for introducing and concluding dialogue

Resources

A collection of stories featuring dialogue. Enlarged text extracts from a selection of these.
Copymasters 1 & 2. Homework 1.

Assessment
At the end of this theme is the pupil able to:
- identify and comment on 'voices' used in the telling of a story;
- understand conventions for the layout and punctuation of speech, and use them as a guide when reading;
- begin using these conventions in own writing;
- identify and use different sentence types (statement, question, exclamation) and the related punctuation marks;
- choose from range of verbs for introducing dialogue?

Lesson 1

Whole class

Explain that in this unit the children will be investigating the use, layout and punctuation of dialogue in stories, and using it in their own writing. Check that everyone understands the term 'dialogue'.
Display and read to the children an enlarged text extract from a story consisting of narrative text and dialogue between two or three characters. *Ask: Who is speaking here? How can we tell?* Work through the text using different-coloured pens to underline or highlight words spoken by each of the characters and to differentiate these from the narrative text. Circle phrases – *e.g. 'said Tom'* – that indicate who is talking. Identify and discuss the function of the narrative text, *e.g. to describe and comment on setting and action.*
Organise a 'choral' reading of the text in which words spoken by the characters and the narrative text are assigned to groups of children.

If there is time, repeat with an extract in which the balance between narrative and dialogue and the number of characters is different.

Group and independent work
Organise groups of children to plan and rehearse dramatised readings of story extracts that include narrative and dialogue. Some groups could make and use simple puppets.

Differentiation
Low Attainers – mark up the beginning of the text in different colours.
High Attainers – work with more complex and challenging texts, *e.g. in which indicators of speaker are not always provided.*

Plenary
Ask groups to introduce their reading by explaining who speaks in it; then present it to the class.
Identify and discuss differences in ways in which dialogue is handled in the texts read.

Lesson 2

Whole class

Revise statements, questions and exclamations by writing up and explaining examples of each, drawing attention to function, typical sentence structures and punctuation. Ask children to read them aloud with appropriate expression.
If the text(s) from Lesson 1 includes these three types of sentence: statement, question and exclamation, re-read it; if not read another that does. Identify examples of each type, and read them aloud together. Identify whether they are in the narrative or the dialogue.
Ask the children to imagine a familiar situation *e.g. going swimming* and the kind of things that might be said. Give them a few minutes to write one example of each type of sentence. Swap with a partner and check each other's work.
Share sentences as a class, taking each type in turn.

Write some up as speech bubbles, emphasising appropriate punctuation. Read with appropriate expression.

Group and independent work
Read story extracts; identify and record examples of statements, questions and exclamation in dialogue.
Write sets of each type, related to some other situation.

Differentiation
Low Attainers – Copymaster 1: demarcate statements, questions and exclamations with the appropriate punctuation marks; continue the dialogue.
High Attainers – write linked sequences of statement, question and exclamation.

Plenary
Share and discuss examples of sentence types found in reading.
Ask children who have written sequences of statements, questions and exclamation to perform with a partner. Ask the rest of the class to identify each type.

Lesson 3

Whole class

Read or re-read an enlarged text consisting mainly of dialogue. Ask: *How do we know who says what? When one person stops talking and another begins?*
Draw attention to and highlight conventions for the punctuation and layout of dialogue:
- **speech marks around words actually spoken.**
  Reinforce this by asking children to say only these words, and by recording them in speech bubbles. Introduce the term 'speech marks'.
- **paragraphing of dialogue:** new speaker, new line.
- **use of capital letters to indicate start of direct speech.**

Use speech bubbles to write up a very short exchange of dialogue between two named characters; these could be based on sentences from the previous lesson. Ask children to rewrite this on their whiteboards, using the conventions just described.
Explain and model the writing of this text, asking

questions to emphasise the key points. *What punctuation mark do we need now? Where do I start writing now?* Discuss possibilities for wording and placement of phrases such as: *said Tom, Zuli said.*

Group and independent work

Suggest a situation, *e.g. child and parent arguing about bedtime.* Pairs of children improvise short conversations, then write them down using speech bubbles and/or conventional dialogue.

Differentiation

Low Attainers – record a conversation on audiocassette; write in speech bubbles first, then change to dialogue.
High Attainers – use dialogue to write a more extended conversation.

Plenary

Display the written conversations round the room, and give children a few minutes to read them.
Choose some pairs to 'perform' these conversations.
Choose texts which highlight correct and incorrect use of conventions; identify and talk through.

Lesson 4

Whole class

Display one of the texts read in previous lessons and read it till you reach the first point at which a word is used to set up dialogue – *e.g. he said, said Tom.* Explain the function of this word, and ask children to read on and record other examples.
Compile a list of all the different words used for this purpose, and highlight them on the text. Prompt children to think of other words that describe different ways of speaking – *e.g. shout, whisper* – and different kinds of utterance – *e.g. reply, order, ask.* Discuss the meaning of each word, and go round the class asking children to say something in the tone of voice suggested by each word. Extend the list.
Identify the different positions that these phrases can occupy in the dialogue: introducing or concluding it, or inserted in the middle. If they are not all represented in

the text, rewrite some sentences, placing them at different points.
Check the spelling of these words, identifying common letter strings, similarities with other words, etc.

Group and independent work

Children read other stories or extracts, and record words used to set up dialogue. Write sentences using words other than 'said' for dialogue.

Differentiation

Low Attainers – prepare a cloze activity, with gaps for words to introduce dialogue.
High Attainers – Copymaster 2: complete text by adding punctuation marks and words for dialogue.

Plenary

Share or add any new words to the list of words for dialogue. Discuss their meaning.
Ask children to say sentences of dialogue they have written in a tone of voice that matches the word.

Lesson 5

Whole class

Choose a familiar story – *e.g. a traditional tale* – or develop one from the conversations improvised in previous Lesson 3 or 4.
Together, plan the first few episodes of this story, focusing on character, for example two characters joined by a third. Quickly review different ways of beginning stories, and tell the children that this story is going to open with dialogue. Decide who is going to speak first, to whom, and roughly the kind of thing that they will say. Give the children a few minutes of time-out to compose an opening sentence of dialogue. Share and write up some possibilities, and choose one.
Talk through and demonstrate the conventions for punctuating and setting out the sentence, revisiting the teaching points from Lesson 3.

Use shared writing techniques to draft the first episode of the story, including as much dialogue as possible.

Group and independent work

Children write their own version of a familiar story, focusing on the use of dialogue. This would work well as a group writing activity, in which children improvise the conversation and then share the writing.

Differentiation

Low Attainers – continue and develop the story begun in whole-class work.
High Attainers – challenge the children to write a story that consists entirely – or almost entirely – of dialogue.

Plenary

Ask children to present dramatised readings of their stories. Discuss the use of dialogue together.
Monitor the children's writing to identify aspects of punctuation and layout of dialogue that are proving difficult. Explain and model correct usage.

Theme 2) Fiction and non-fiction

Objectives

Text level:
- 16 understand the distinction between fiction and non-fiction
- 17 notice differences in the style and structure of fiction and non-fiction writing
- 18 locate information using contents, headings and sub-headings
- 21 make a simple record of information

Sentence level:
- 1 use awareness of grammar and other strategies in reading
- 9 notice and investigate a range of devices for presenting texts

Word level:
- 6 use independent spelling strategies
- 13 collect new words from reading
- 14 infer the meaning of unknown words from context

Resources

A range of fiction and non-fiction texts on the same or closely related subjects, *e.g. animals.* Include examples which exemplify the language and layout features of each genre, some with challenging vocabulary. Enlarged text extracts from these, including the contents list from the main non-fiction text.
Copymasters 3 & 4. Homework 2.

Assessment

At the end of this theme is the pupil able to:
- distinguish between fiction and non-fiction, explaining their reasons with reference to the characteristic features of each;
- use a range of reading strategies to work out the meaning of unfamiliar words;
- raise simple questions about a topic, and use non-fiction texts to look for the answers;
- record information in a range of simple ways?

Lesson 1

Whole class

Display an enlarged text extract from a story which includes some words that are likely to be unfamiliar. Ask the children to read it independently, and to record words that are difficult to read and/or new to them. Then read the text together. When you reach an unfamiliar word, explain and prompt use of a range of reading strategies to decode it and work out its meaning. *Ask: Is that a word that you had trouble with? What strategies did you use?* Compile a list of these words.
Ask: What kind of writing is this? How can we tell? Identify and discuss features of fiction writing, *e.g. chronological ordering of events, use of dialogue, imagined (though usually possible) events happening to particular characters, use of past tense, layout in running text paragraphs, use of pictures to illustrate and extend the text.*

Discuss how this kind of text is intended to be read: from the beginning through to the end.

Group and independent work
Children read other fiction texts, noting words that are new to them and/or difficult to read. Copy out the sentence that includes the most problematic word.

Differentiation
Low Attainers – work with the children in the context of guided reading, focusing on strategies for new/difficult words.
High Attainers – Copymaster 3: work out the meaning of less familiar words in a story extract.

Plenary
Write up some of the sentences which children identified; read together, reinforcing reading strategies and discussing the meaning of new words.
Remind children of the features of fiction writing; ask them to comment on their use in the extracts they read.

Lesson 2

Whole class

Choose a subject similar to that in the story extract read in the previous lesson, *e.g. about a different animal, or the same characters in a different situation.* Remind the children of some techniques for planning stories, and give them a few minutes to record ideas. Share these, and choose one idea (or combination of ideas) to develop together.
Use shared writing techniques to begin drafting the story. As the writing proceeds, focus children's attention on the features of layout and language identified in Lesson 1, especially sequence of events in time, consistent use of past tense, and paragraphing.
Focus also on word choice, *e.g. by introducing less usual words and explaining what they mean.* Ask the children to try writing them. Share attempts, and use as the starting point for developing spelling strategies, *e.g. drawing attention to common letter strings and word endings;*

using knowledge of different ways of spelling long vowel phonemes.

Group and independent work
Children write the beginning of a story with a similar subject. Set them the target of using some interesting and less usual words, and trying to spell them independently.

Differentiation
Low Attainers – continue the story begun in whole-class work.
High Attainers – start by listing interesting, less usual words that could be used in writing about their chosen subject.

Plenary
Share new words, orally; work together to spell them, using a range of strategies.
Read beginnings of some stories; discuss word choice and use of features of fiction writing.

Lesson 3

Whole class

Choose a non-fiction text on the same subject as the fiction in Lesson 1, and including typical features of language and layout. Prepare an enlarged text version and cover up some content words, including a few that are likely to be unfamiliar.

Read this with the children; pause for them to speculate about the hidden words. Prompt use of contextual and grammatical information. List new and/or specialist words. Ask: *What kind of writing is this? How is it different from the text we read in the first lesson?* Give children time out to share ideas with a partner. In whole-class discussion, identify and discuss:
- the use of headings and sub-headings;
- the use of illustrations, charts, diagrams with labels and/or captions;
- how the information is organised (not chronologically);
- what it is about, drawing out the idea that it is general rather than specific.

Introduce or revise the term non-fiction to describe this kind of text.

Group and independent work

Children read extracts from other non-fiction books; identify unfamiliar and/or difficult words and list the organisational and presentational features used. Display a list of these (see opposite) for children to refer to.

Differentiation

Low Attainers – Copymaster 4: chart for recording presentational features and specialist or unusual words in a non-fiction text.

High Attainers – Copymaster 4: in addition, write a short comment about the non-fiction book.

Plenary

Select sentences including new and/or difficult words; write them up; talk through reading strategies to decode them and work out their meanings.
Ask children to comment on the features used in the books they have read.

Lesson 4

Whole class

Return to the non-fiction text from the previous lesson. Ask children how it should be read; draw out the idea that readers do not have to start at the beginning but can use the headings to help them choose the parts they want to read. Contrast this with fiction text.

Pose a question that is answered in the text. Give the children a few minutes to read independently to find the answer.

Identify the answer and highlight the relevant part of the text. Explain and demonstrate how to use headings and sub-headings to locate the information. Repeat with other questions.

Show the book from which the extract is taken, and an enlarged version of the contents page. Explain that this shows how the information in the book is organised. Prompt children to raise questions which the book might

answer; write up some of these. Taking each in turn, ask: *Which part of the book will we need to read?* Demonstrate the process of looking for information that answers the question, focusing on the use of page numbers.

Group and independent work

Children choose an information book (on the same broad subject); raise and write down three questions that they think it will answer. Then use organisational devices to look for relevant information. Record the answers.

Differentiation

Low Attainers – guide choice of book, and provide questions that you know it answers.

High Attainers – write a short account of how they found the answer to one of their questions.

Plenary

Ask children to share questions that they successfully answered; prompt them to describe what organisational devices they used to find it.

Lesson 5

Whole class

Give groups or individuals a few minutes to share information they have gained about the subject with children who worked with a different book; to identify the most interesting facts, and record them. Share as a class.

Choose an aspect of the subject, and discuss ways that they could record the information; prompt children to draw on the range of forms used in the non-fiction texts read.

Choose an appropriate, simple form, *e.g. labelled picture or diagram; picture with caption; a few sentences under a series of headings and sub-headings.*

Use shared writing techniques to draft the text (sketch in any illustrations quickly). Draw the children's attention to the relevant features of non-fiction writing, revising teaching points from Lesson 3.

Repeat this process for other information, using a different form.

Group and independent work

Children choose information that interests them, and record it using one of the forms encountered in reading non-fiction texts and/or in whole-class work above.

Differentiation

Low Attainers – represent information in a different form, e.g. as a chart or list of key words.

High Attainers – encourage children to use a form with more extended text.

Plenary

Ask children to swap their work; give them a couple of minutes for reading. Then ask some to present the work to the class, explaining how their partner has presented the information. Discuss the range of forms, and their suitability for different kinds of information.

Theme 3) Non-chronological reports

Objectives

Text level:
- 17 notice differences in style and structure of fiction and non-fiction writing
- 18 locate information, using headings and sub-headings
- 20 read information passages, and identify main points
- 22 write simple non-chronological reports from known information

Sentence level:
- 10 identify boundaries between sentences in reading and writing
- 11 write in complete sentences
- 12 demarcate the end of a sentence with a full stop and start a new one with a capital letter

Word level:
- 10 recognise and spell common prefixes
- 11 use knowledge of prefixes to generate new words from root words, especially antonyms
- 12 use the term 'prefix'

Resources

Non-fiction books written, wholly or in part, as non-chronological reports, using headings and sub-headings to indicate how information is organised. Enlarged text extracts of non-chronological reports. Copymasters 5 & 6. Homework 3.

Assessment

At the end of this theme is the pupil able to:
- identify and discuss the simpler structural and stylistic features of non-chronological reports;
- identify key points in reading, and use a range of strategies to record them;
- plan and write a simple non-chronological report, using language and structural features;
- write in complete sentences, and demarcate them with full stops and capital letters;
- recognise words consisting of prefix plus root in reading and writing, and spell common prefixes?

Lesson 1

Whole class

Show the class the cover and a few pages from a non-fiction book in which information is organised non-chronologically. Identify and discuss the information it provides and how (broadly) this is organised. Draw attention to role of main headings in indicating this. Read an enlarged text version of a double-page spread from the book. Prompt children to explain how the information is organised, identifying the structure of headings and sub-headings and the focus of each section. Ask: *What section would you read if you wanted to find out about ...?* Explain and demonstrate use of headings to locate information.

Ask individuals or small groups to read the first sentence while the rest of the class listens and follows. *Ask: did they stop at the right place? How did they know when they had reached the end of the first sentence?* Revise use of full stops and capital letters to mark sentence boundaries. Ask others to read on a sentence at a time.

Group and independent work

Copymaster 6: Children explore the structure of non-chronological texts by sequencing sections and headings or by dividing continuous text into sections with headings, where possible working with computer text.

Differentiation

Low Attainers – Copymaster 5: cut out and sequence sections of text and headings to make a coherent report.
High Attainers – Copymaster 6: organise text into sections and write appropriate headings.

Plenary

Re-read the enlarged text. Prompt discussion of the kind of information it provides, focusing on the idea that the author states general facts and does not (usually) express a personal view.

Lesson 2

Whole class

Choose a double-page spread from a non-chronological report in which there is a clear distinction between main ideas and supporting detail. Read an enlarged text version with the children. Identify and discuss similarities and differences with the non-chronological text read in Lesson 1.

Focus on the first paragraph or section; prompt children to identify the main idea. Ask them to work in pairs to pick out the main ideas in the rest of the text and find a way of recording them.

Work through the text together, section by section, identifying the main idea in each. Explain and demonstrate a range of ways of recording this:
- highlighting key words and phrases;
- listing main ideas in note form;
- (if appropriate) as a chart in which information is organised under headings.

Group and independent work

Children read other non-chronological reports, and identify and record main ideas using one of the strategies modelled in whole-class work. Towards the end of this phase, swap work with others working with the same text; discuss whether they have identified the same points.

Differentiation

Low Attainers – highlight main ideas on a photocopied text.
High Attainers – record main ideas by writing an organised list.

Plenary

Share a text that has been highlighted; read through, asking children whether the key ideas have been correctly identified.

Work together to record these as a list; focus on brevity; look for ways of organising points in the list.

Lesson 3
Whole class

In this lesson the focus is on word-level work with prefixes. Prepare for it by writing cards with the prefixes *un, mis* and *dis* and words to which they can be added. If possible, return to the shared texts from Lessons 1 and/or 2 and highlight words beginning with common prefixes. Ask children what they notice about these words; write them out, drawing a vertical line to separate prefix from root. Introduce and explain the term prefix. Ask children to write other words beginning with these prefixes. Compile a list for each.

Write up words beginning with other common prefixes; ask children to write down two words that begin with each, and share as before. Explain the meaning of each prefix.

Display the root and prefix cards. Ask children to make words by putting them together. Read and identify the meaning of the resulting words. Write them up in pairs of opposites.

Group and independent work
Children go on a five-minute prefix hunt, reading texts and listing words with prefixes. Write up a list of common prefixes: ask children to write five words that begin with each.

Differentiation
Low Attainers – use the prefix *un* to write more pairs of opposites.
High Attainers – write lists of words that can be formed by adding different prefixes to the same root, *e.g. misused, reused, unused, disused.*

Plenary
Ask children to share any words they found beginning with prefixes that were not discussed in whole-class work. Share roots words to which several prefixes can be added; identify meaning of resulting words.

Lesson 4
Whole class

Explain that the children are going to work together to write a report about their school for new pupils. Give pairs of children time out to share ideas about the information that should be included. Share ideas as a class; record them, beginning to sort and organise them.

Review this information, and discuss ways in which it could be organised. Ask children to write two headings for the report.

Share these, and work together to create a structure of headings and sub-headings. Look for opportunities to explain the focusing and grouping of information about specific subjects, and how this could be organised under sub-headings under the main heading 'Lessons'.

Choose one of the sections, and give children time-out to jot down notes about information to be included. Share and write up. Check for relevance – *Does that belong here?* – and identify places where notes could be briefer.

Group and independent work
Children plan their own non-chronological report about their school by writing headings and sub-headings, working on large sheets of paper (choose a section and make notes for writing it). Encourage them to draw on whole-class work but also to add ideas of their own.

Differentiation
Low Attainers – give children notes for them to organise under two headings; then add ideas of their own.
High Attainers – plan one large section of the report in detail, with sub-headings.

Plenary
Share some plans. Revisit issues of organisation discussed in whole-class work. Refocus and rewrite headings as appropriate.

Lesson 5
Whole class

Return to the notes made in the previous lesson. Ask: *what shall we write first in this section?* Discuss possibilities, guiding children to start with the main idea. Frame a simple sentence orally, then write it up; draw attention to the capital letter and full stop.

Use shared writing techniques to compose the rest of the text, prompting children to elaborate on the main idea. From time to time ask the children to write the next sentence; differentiate this by asking high attainers to write the next two sentences. Draw on these contributions to continue the text. Look for opportunities to explain and model how to shape ideas as complete sentences. Remind children also of the language conventions of non-chronological reports, in particular writing in an impersonal style and describing 'what happens' generally rather than 'what happened' on a specific occasion.

Group and independent work
Children write their own non-chronological reports about school, using the plans and notes they made in Lesson 4. This provides an opportunity for more extended writing, in subsequent Literacy Hours and/or outside this context.

Differentiation
Low Attainers – write the two sections that they organised and made notes for in Lesson 4.
High Attainers – write the section with sub-headings that they planned in Lesson 4.

Plenary
Read work in progress and finished reports (including headings) to the class. Focus discussion on key teaching points: especially organisation and giving information about how things work generally.

Theme 4) Organisation and presentation of information

Objectives

Text level:
- 17 notice differences in the style and structure of fiction and non-fiction writing
- 18 locate information, using contents, index and headings
- 19 compare the way information is presented
- 21 make a simple record of information

Sentence level:
- 9 notice and investigate a range of ways of presenting texts

Word level:
- 13 collect new words from reading
- 14 infer the meaning of unknown words from context

Resources
A non-fiction book to use as the core text, including contents, index and glossary. Enlarged text versions of these and other pages. A collection of non-fiction books on the same theme, using a variety of devices to present information.
Copymasters 7 & 8. Homework 4.

Assessment
At the end of this theme is the pupil able to:
- understand the function of contents pages and indexes and use them effectively;
- search an information text to find particular items of information, using a range of organisational devices;
- 'read' and interpret information presented in a range of different ways;
- use context to work out the meaning of new words encountered in reading;
- make own record of information using a range of appropriate forms?

Lesson 1

Whole class

Explain that in this unit the children will be investigating how information is organised and presented in non-fiction books. Show children the cover of the 'core' book. Prompt them to predict what information it provides and to discuss ways of reading it. Draw out the idea that readers can choose parts which interest them or which provide answers to their questions.

Give the children time-out to think of questions the book might answer and record them. Share suggestions; choose a few questions that are answered in the book. Read the contents page of the enlarged text; explain that it shows how the book is divided into sections, giving page numbers for each. Show how the contents matches the headings and page numbers in the body of the book.

Focus on the first question. Ask children to read the contents and say which section will provide the answer.

Model the process of finding the right section, using page numbers. Repeat with other questions.

Group and independent work
Working with another book, children raise three questions it might answer; look at the contents page; identify the section likely to provide the answer; find and book mark that section. Read those sections to find the answer.

Differentiation
Low Attainers – give the children some questions related to the contents of their book.
High Attainers – record their work on a three-column chart: question; page number; answer.

Plenary
Help children to share the process of using the contents page to find the right section. Use any problems to extend teaching points.
Show an enlarged contents page again. Read items of information; ask children to identify the section from which they come.

Lesson 2

Whole class

Remind children of work with contents pages. Explain that non-fiction books have another way of helping readers look for information: the index. Show the enlarged text index. Ask them what they notice. Draw out the idea that it is an alphabetically organised list; that the page number(s) indicates where information about that item can be found. Explain that the index helps readers find more detailed information than the contents. Prompt children to raise more questions that the book might answer. Choose one. Identify the key word, and model the process of finding it in the index and looking up the relevant pages. Repeat for other questions. Explain how to scan down lists of words beginning with the same letter, noting second and subsequent letters. To reinforce this, choose a topic, *e.g. animals, vehicles, foods*. Brainstorm and record words belonging in this category; contribute some yourself to ensure that

several begin with the same letter. Give children time-out to begin sorting these words into alphabetical order. Share results; focus on second and subsequent letters.

Group and independent work
Use the index in the non-fiction book to track down information, as in Lesson 1.
Ask each member of the group to write down five words in a category on small pieces of paper; then pool and sort the words into alphabetical order.

Differentiation
Low Attainers – Copymaster 7: alphabetical sorting requiring attention to second letters.
High Attainers – Copymaster 8: alphabetical sorting requiring attention to second and subsequent letters.

Plenary
Brainstorm and record a list of words in the same category that all begin with the same letter; talk through the process of sorting them into alphabetical order.

Lesson 3
Whole class

Display an enlarged text version of a page(s) from the core book, including examples of specialist vocabulary explained in the glossary and other words likely to be unfamiliar. Give the children time to read this independently; ask them to note down any new or difficult words.

Re-read the text together. Pause on new words; talk through and model strategies for inferring their meaning from the context. Explain that in reading non-fiction on an unfamiliar topic, they are likely to meet new words; that many books include a glossary to explain such words.

Show the enlarged text glossary. Explain how it is organised, and use it to check the meaning of the specialist words in the text. Re-read and develop an understanding of the relevant passages.

Choose a specialist word that they have recently met in other curriculum activities; work together to write a glossary entry for this word.

Group and independent work

Read a section from the non-fiction book they used in Lessons 1 and 2. Note specialist words, and look them up in the glossary.

Children write glossary entries for three specialist words related to a personal interest or hobby.

Differentiation

Low Attainers – read a book in which words in the glossary are shown in a different type-face.

High Attainers – try to infer meaning from context; write provisional definition; use glossary to check.

Plenary

Ask children to share interesting specialist words they have met, reading the sentence in which they occur and the glossary entry.

Share glossary entries the children have written; discuss whether meanings are clear to non-specialists.

Lesson 4
Whole class

Display large versions of pages from the core text and other non-fiction books in which information is presented in different ways: as text with headings and sub-headings; as labelled pictures and diagrams; as flow charts or 'cycles' with arrows; as pictures with captions. Start with the picture and caption. Identify and describe it, using the correct terminology. Prompt children to discuss how to 'read' it, in particular looking at how images and words are related and work together. Read the text, and ask children questions which prompt recall and interpretation of information in the words and picture. Repeat for the other forms of presentation; but now give children time to read independently and to note answers to your questions. Share answers. Then check and develop by reading the text together.

Review all the forms discussed; prompt children to discuss what each one is especially good for.

Group and independent work

Children find, 'bookmark' and read examples of these and other forms of presentation in the non-fiction books they have been reading. Choose the one they think provides the most interesting information in the clearest way.

Differentiation

Low Attainers – give the children strips of paper, with names of different forms, to use as bookmarks.

High Attainers – write a short explanation of why the chosen form was clear and interesting.

Plenary

Ask the children to share examples of the forms identified in whole-class work.

Ask if anyone has found other ways of presenting information; share and discuss these.

Lesson 5
Whole class

Choose a subject with which the children are familiar from work in other curriculum areas; for this purpose, animals would be ideal, because information about this subject can be presented in many different ways. Use a mind-map to identify areas within this subject, *e.g. body parts, life cycles*.

Choose one of these areas, and discuss together how information about it could be presented, referring back to the range of forms from Lesson 4. Repeat for another area of information.

Divide the class into groups, assigning an area of information to each; differentiate by asking lower attainers to work on one of the areas already discussed. Give the class time-out to talk about how best to present the information. Then ask each group to share their ideas, giving their reasons.

Choose one to develop together, using shared writing techniques; sketch any pictorial elements.

Group and independent work

Children work in groups from whole-class phase to present information about their aspect of the subject in their chosen form. They could work together to produce a joint outcome or individually, each producing their own version.

Differentiation

Low Attainers – choose from forms which are largely pictorial or graphic.

High Attainers – experiment with presenting information in two different forms; choose and develop the one which works best

Plenary

Share work. Ask children to explain why they chose to present the information in this way. Develop discussion of how various forms work and their suitability for different kinds of information.

Theme 5) Playscripts

Objectives

Text level:
- 4 read, prepare and present playscripts
- 5 recognise the key differences between prose and playscript
- 14 write simple playscripts based on own reading and oral work

Sentence level:
- 2 take account of grammar and punctuation when reading aloud
- 6 secure knowledge of question marks and exclamation marks in reading and use in own writing
- 9 notice and investigate a range of devices for presenting texts

Resources

Prose and playscript versions of the same story, e.g. a traditional tale. Choose a playscript which does not include a 'narrator'. Enlarged text extracts and extracts for annotation from both genres. Unpunctuated extracts from stories (leave speech marks in); if possible, also replace capitals with lower case letters at the start of sentences. Look for extracts which include examples of all three sentence types, e.g. in the dialogue. Cards showing full stops, question marks and exclamation marks.
Copymasters 9 & 10. Homework 5.

Assessment
At the end of this theme is the pupil able to:
- identify and discuss the differences between prose and playscript, considering layout, language and treatment;
- work with others to plan and rehearse a read-aloud performance of a playscript;
- use punctuation marks as a guide when reading;
- use full stops, question marks and exclamation marks to demarcate sentences in own writing?

Lesson 1

Whole class

Display an enlarged text extract from a traditional tale. Ask the children if they can tell what kind of writing it is just by the way it looks on the page. Once they have identified it as a story, ask them how they could tell. Draw attention to paragraphing, presentation of dialogue with speech marks, and use of illustrations. Read the text together. Ask questions to develop and extend children's understanding of features of narrative texts, e.g: *How does the author tell you about the characters? Where is the story happening? How does he/she show you what people say? How is the text organised?* Annotate and mark up the text to show and name these features. Ask the children to join in as you read the story. Pause to work on phrasing and intonation. Demonstrate how to use punctuation; identify what full stops, question marks and exclamation marks 'tell' the reader. Highlight these in the text.

Organise the whole-class and groups to re-read sentences and passages independently.

Group and independent work
Children read other story extracts, and mark up and annotate them to show key features of narrative prose. Write up a list for reference. Then plan and rehearse group reading for a performance of the text.

Differentiation
Low Attainers – mark up the text by highlighting the narrative and dialogue in different colours.
High Attainers – plan a dramatised reading, with children taking 'parts' as characters and narrator.

Plenary
Give one child in each group cards showing a full stop, a question mark and an exclamation mark. Ask him/her to hold up the appropriate card at the end of each sentence as they read their extract to the class.

Lesson 2

Whole class

Read together the beginning of an enlarged text extract from a playscript version of the story from Lesson 1 (leave the list of characters and other preliminaries for Lesson 4).
Ask children what they notice. Confirm that it is the same story. Read on to the end. Ask: *What's different about this way of telling the story?* Give the children time-out to share ideas with a partner. Then discuss as a class. Explain aspects of content (story told through dialogue and action; no narrator) and presentation (character's name followed by what she/he says; different print styles to indicate different kinds of text; stage directions). Highlight and annotate the text to show these features. Ask children to read the text independently, searching for different punctuation marks. They could come out to mark these on the text.

Re-read the extract together, again developing intonation and phrasing, using punctuation as a guide. Draw attention to stage directions indicating expression, e.g. *'softly', 'whispering'.*

Group and independent work
Working as a group, children read and discuss an extract from a playscript, and choose one feature to tell the class about. They plan and rehearse a performance.

Differentiation
Low Attainers – continue reading the playscript used in whole-class work.
High Attainers – show children how to mark up the text with notes to guide performance.

Plenary
Share features of playscripts the children have noticed; develop in relation to the enlarged text. Ask one or two groups to present their performances. Comment on and discuss, picking up points about playscript conventions.

Lesson 3
Whole class

Display an enlarged text version of an unpunctuated story extract. Read the text together; after a couple of sentences ask the children what's missing. Discuss why the absence of punctuation marks at the end of sentences makes it harder to read.

Read the text to the children without pausing between sentences; ask them to put their hands up when they think a new sentence begins; re-read together to identify this point exactly. Decide whether a full stop, question mark or exclamation mark should be used; read again to check expression. Circle the first letter of the following sentence to show that it should be a capital. Re-read the edited text together, using punctuation to guide intonation and phrasing.

Explain other ways of marking words, especially in dialogue, to show expression and emphasis, *e.g. using*

capital letters and different print styles. Look for places in the text where words could be presented in these ways.

Group and independent work

Children edit a story text, adding missing punctuation marks and changing words to show emphasis and expression.

Differentiation

Low Attainers – Copymaster 9: punctuate short dialogue, adding appropriate punctuation marks.
High Attainers – Copymaster 10: edit a longer and more challenging text.

Plenary

Ask children to share sentences in which they changed the style of a word for emphasis. Write up and discuss examples.

Ask a group to read the text they edited, saying the punctuation marks, with one child holding up appropriate cards (see Lesson 1).

Lesson 4
Whole class

Show an enlarged text version of the preliminaries *e.g. the description of setting of first scene from the playscript read in Lesson 2.*

Read the list of characters; ask children to identify what it is. If this includes other information *e.g. 'a little girl', 'wizard',* discuss its purpose. Discuss why lists like this are not needed at the beginning of stories.

Read the description of setting; discuss information it provides. Identify any unusual features of style, *e.g. note-form with verbless sentences (A shoe-maker's cottage. Early morning).*

Choose a familiar traditional tale. Give children, working in pairs, time-out to list the characters in the story. Differentiate by asking groups to do this in any order; in order of appearance; in order of importance. Share and discuss lists. Discuss whether information about the characters should be added; experiment with this.

Identify where the story begins, and ask children to write a short description of this setting. Share contributions; draw on them to write a joint description.

Group and independent work

Groups choose a traditional tale that they know well; write a list of characters, and a description of the setting for the first scene.

Differentiation

Low Attainers – from the text used in whole-class work, choose an episode from later in the story; list the characters and describe the setting.
High Attainers – list the characters in order of appearance; add information about who they are.

Plenary

Ask children to read descriptions of setting; ask others to identify the story. Discuss whether it provides the necessary information.

Write up a list of characters in any order; work together to reorder.

Lesson 5
Whole class

Explain that the children are now going to work together to write the beginning of a playscript version of the traditional tale chosen in the previous lesson. Identify who will be in the first scene; who will speak first and to whom; what they will say.

Organise children into groups of appropriate size, and give them a few minutes to improvise this scene. Ask some groups to present their improvisation. Discuss. Draw on this to draft the playscript, using shared writing techniques. Draw attention to features of presentation and treatment highlighted in Lesson 2. Prompt children in particular to identify points at which stage directions would be useful. From time to time, give children time-out to compose a sentence of dialogue or a stage direction; share, and draw on for the joint text.

During the writing, also highlight demarcation of sentences, and whether full stops, question marks or exclamation marks should be used.

Group and independent work

Children write a playscript version of the first scene of the traditional tale that they chose in Lesson 4, using conventions of presentation and language.

Differentiation

Low Attainers – improvise and record the first few exchanges; produce a written version.
High Attainers – encourage children to make full use of stage directions.

Plenary

Ask groups to read one line which includes a stage direction, and to perform just that line following it. Invite groups to perform their playscripts. Discuss: *Is the story clear? Can you tell which character is which?*

Theme 6 Poems of observation and the senses

Objectives

Text level:
- 6 read aloud and recite poems, comparing different views of the same subject; discuss choice of words and phrases
- 7 distinguish between rhyming and non-rhyming poetry and comment on impact of layout
- 8 express views about a poem
- 12 collect words and phrases to write poems; design simple patterns with words

Sentence level:
- 3 recognise the function of verbs in sentences

Word level:
- 2 identify, blend and segment phonemes
- 17 generate synonyms

Resources

Collections of poems based on observation and the sense, including sets of poems about the same or similar subjects and examples of both rhyming and non-rhyming poetry. Thematic anthologies of poetry. Enlarged text versions of selected poems.
Copymasters 11 & 12. Homework 6.

Assessment

At the end of this theme is the pupil able to:
- identify and comment on significant aspects of content and language in poems;
- join in discussion of poems, expressing and explaining their views;
- read and write sets of rhyming words;
- generate and choose between words for writing about a particular subject, considering impact and distinguishing between synonyms?

Lesson 1

Whole class

Prepare for this lesson by choosing a rhyming poem, and covering up the second rhyme in each pair.
Explain that in this unit they will be reading and writing poems which describe things. Choose a short rhyming poem, read and re-read it to the children without showing the text. Give children a brief time-out to share first impressions with a partner; then discuss as a class. Prompt by asking: *What is the poet saying? What words do you remember? What did you notice about the sounds of the poem?*
Read an enlarged text version of the poem. Pause for children to work out the 'missing' rhyming words. Write it up. Ask: *where is the rhyme? – in the later part of each word?* Underline these parts. Note whether the spelling patterns are the same (food/mood) or different (food/rude).

Ask children to think of other words that belong to these rhyming sets, and add them to the list. Look for opportunities to extend knowledge of patterns for spelling phonemes, especially long vowels.

Group and independent work

Children read other rhyming poems; list the words that rhyme; add others. Practise reading the poem aloud.

Differentiation

Low Attainers – read a poem in simple rhyming couplets; list the rhyming pairs; add one more word to each.
High Attainers – Copymaster 11: list rhyming words in a poem with a more complex pattern; add others to each list.

Plenary

Share pairs of rhyming words children have found; work together to extend the list; note spelling patterns. Choose children to read or recite their poem; discuss.

Lesson 2

Whole class

Choose a poem, on the same subject as that in Lesson 1, which does not rhyme but has strong elements of patterning. Prepare for this lesson by covering up some words or lines where this pattern is repeated, and writing out all or some of the poem as prose.
Read an enlarged text version to the children. Identify the pattern(s). Give children time-out to invent and write down the 'missing' words or lines. Share ideas; identify ones which do/do not follow the pattern. Reveal the words and lines in the poem.
Ask children to look at the words that end each line. What do they notice? Confirm the idea that the poem does not rhyme.
Display the prose version of the poem, and read it with the children. Discuss differences, *e.g. in the way you read it, in its power and interest, in the impact of the patterning.*

Give children a couple of minutes to re-read the original poem, and to try to learn it (or some of it) by heart. Ask volunteers to have a try at reciting it.

Group and independent work

Children read other non-rhyming (but patterned) poems. Decide on one interesting thing about the poem to share with the class. Children learn as much of it as they can by heart.

Differentiation

Low Attainers – Copymaster 12: rewrite a prose version of a non-rhyming poem, restoring the original layout.
High Attainers – find, in anthologies, two non-rhyming poems with different patterns.

Plenary

Choose children to introduce and comment on non-rhyming poems, and to try reciting them from memory. Write up lines to illustrate patterning and layout.

Lesson 3
Whole class

Prepare for this lesson by choosing another poem (rhyming or non-rhyming) on the same subject, and which includes striking choices of vocabulary. Prepare for the lesson by covering up a selection of these words. Read an enlarged text version of the poem. Pause at each missing word. Identify those which must be verbs. Prompt children to speculate about what the word might be. List possibilities. Re-read, inserting suggested synonyms, checking that they make sense and considering their effect. Reveal the original word. Discuss why they think the poet chose it.

Re-read the complete poem. Ask children whether it is rhyming or non-rhyming. If it is rhyming, identify the rhyming words; investigate spelling patterns. If it is not, identify and discuss other patterns, and how the poem is organised and set out in lines.

Group and independent work
Make available other poems which include unusual, powerful, interesting words. Children choose and read one of these; list or highlight words that catch their attention; underline any that are verbs; and choose one word to tell the rest of the class about.

Differentiation
Low Attainers – choose words from the enlarged text poems read in this unit.
High Attainers – list the verbs in the poem; list others that the poet might have used instead.

Plenary
Share lines with powerful, interesting words; write some down. Discuss the meaning and impact of the words; identify other words that the poet might have used. Substitute, read, and discuss effect.

Lesson 4
Whole class

Prompt children to share experiences and ideas about the subject of the three poems read. Then re-read the poems, and leave them all displayed for children to re-read and refer to.

Ask children to identify some similarities and differences between the poems. Model sentence structures which express this, *e.g. X and Y both ...; All three poems ...; X has ... but Y...*

Give children, working in pairs, time-out to compare the poems, and to share views about which one they like most.

Lead a whole class discussion, focusing first on comparing the poems in detail. Prompt children to consider different aspects: what the poet says, structure, word choice, mood (serious, humorous).

Focus next on preferences, prompting children to explain their views by referring to particular words in and aspects of the text. Encourage others to comment, presenting opposing views or qualifications.

Group and independent work
Children review the poems they have read in this unit, and choose a favourite. They write a short explanation of what they like about it and why; learn the poem by heart.

Differentiation
Low Attainers – prepare a simple writing frame with sentence starters to support this activity
High Attainers – encourage children to refer to the text, *e.g. giving them a checklist of things to write about.*

Plenary
Choose children to recite their favourite poem, and then to read their explanation of what they like. Prompt others to share their views; look for opportunities to extend knowledge of aspects of poetic style and form.

Lesson 5
Whole class

Give pairs of children an object (of the same kind), *e.g. pebbles, shells, dried leaves, small sponges, grapes.* Give them time to share ideas about this object, and to list on their whiteboards words that they could use to describe it. Prompt and focus this by asking them to think about information provided by different senses. Write up a list of these, or which ever are appropriate for the object! After a few minutes, share and write up words. Introduce less familiar words yourself, and prompt children to think of synonyms.

Read and review these words; ask individuals to choose the three that they think are most interesting and powerful. Share ideas. Is there agreement about this? Choose and display a poem (read in whole class or group work) with a strong, simple, small-scale pattern, *e.g. repetitive phrases, simple comparisons, sentences with the same structure.* Draw on the word bank to write lines with this pattern about the object they have been describing.

If there is time, repeat this process with other patterns.

Group and independent work
Children work, individually or in groups, to write more lines, following the patterns modelled in whole-class work.

Differentiation
Low Attainers – each child writes one or two lines; then pool and organise them to make a group poem.
High Attainers – choose another pattern from their own reading in this unit.

Plenary
Ask children to read their poems. Discuss patterning and choice of words.

Plan and organise ways of collecting poems to make a class anthology.

Theme 7) Story settings

Objectives

Text level:
- 1 compare a range of story settings
- 9 generate ideas relevant to a topic
- 11 develop the use of settings in own stories
- 15 begin to organise stories into paragraphs

Word level:
- 7 practise new spellings
- 13 collect new words from reading
- 17 generate synonyms for high frequency words
- 18 use the term 'synonym'

Resources

A collection of stories in which setting plays an important part; enlarged text versions of descriptive passages from these stories, including some adventurous and unusual vocabulary.
Copymasters 13 & 14. Homework 7.

Assessment

At the end of this theme is the pupil able to:
- discuss and compare the settings of stories, identifying words and phrases used to describe them;
- write short but detailed and vivid descriptions of setting, considering word choice, especially distinguishing between words with similar meanings;
- write a story in which the element of setting is highlighted;
- identify and discuss distinctions between synonyms;
- identify new words, work out and discuss their meanings, and spell them accurately?

Lesson 1

Whole class

Explain that in this unit the children will be exploring the places in which stories are set, writing their own descriptions of places, and using them in a story. Read an extract from a familiar story, and ask the children where the action takes place; repeat for stories with other settings. Include examples in which the action moves from one setting to another. Write up matching titles and settings, e.g. 'Owl Babies'. In the park. Give children, working in pairs, time-out to write down more titles and setting(s). Share ideas, and add to the list. Categorise and sort, e.g. school, countryside, seaside. Focus on one or two stories in which setting plays a significant part. Chart changes in setting graphically, e.g. as a flow-chart. Develop the discussion by prompting children to describe and explain how the action of the story and characters' behaviour is affected by setting.

List and discuss the meaning of any less common words encountered in reading and discussing settings.

Group and independent work

Choose and re-read all or part of a book they know and like; write a stand-up label which describes place(s) where the story is set. Choose and bookmark a page where setting is described in pictures and/or text.

Differentiation

Low Attainers – photocopy a picture showing setting; children write a short caption and labels.
High Attainers – choose and describe a story with multiple settings.

Plenary

Drawing on independent work, children describe the setting(s) of their chosen stories, showing the chosen page. Prompt them to categorise and compare settings, and to talk about how they affect action and character. Organise a display of labelled books.

Lesson 2

Whole class

Read an enlarged text extract including description of a familiar setting, preferably from the beginning of the story. Ask children where the story is set. Ask them, individually or in pairs, to note down on their whiteboards the words and phrases that indicate the setting. Share; underline or highlight the enlarged text. If there are illustrations, discuss the part they play in presenting the setting, in particular what they add to information in the text.
Ask: *What's happening so far in the story? What might happen next? What is unlikely to happen here?* Draw out links between action and setting.
Choose a word, *e.g. seaside*. Ask children to search their vocabularies and write down words to do with this setting, *e.g. beach, sand, waves, rocks*. Share and record ideas. Repeat with other words if time.
Choose from the list (or introduce) a word for which there are several synonyms, *e.g. street*. Prompt children

to suggest these, *e.g. road, path, lane, track*. Identify and discuss differences in meaning; introduce and explain the term synonym.

Group and independent work

Children generate lists of words to do with other settings, presenting them on large sheets of paper as web diagrams.
Write a list of synonyms for 'house'.

Differentiation

Low Attainers – Copymaster 13: draw lines to link sets of synonyms that describe similar places and kinds of weather.
High Attainers – write definitions of synonyms and/or use them in sentences which show their meaning.

Plenary

Share synonyms for house; identify and discuss differences in meaning.
Work together to make a class web diagram of words to do with settings, extending the range of vocabulary.

Lesson 3

Whole class

Prepare an enlarged text version of the opening of a story with a different setting, including description which makes use of adventurous and unusual words; cover up these words and others which relate to setting.

Read the text with the children, pausing for them to suggest what the hidden words might be; check back and read on to see if the suggestions make sense grammatically and contextually. Reveal the word letter by letter, checking phonic and graphic match.

Write up a list of the less common words; identify and discuss their meaning.

Talk through and demonstrate strategies for learning the spelling of these new words. Practise together using the 'look, say, cover, write, check' method.

Discuss how the story begins: with description of setting/ action/someone speaking? Compare with openings of familiar stories. Identify and record range of ways in which stories can begin; identify favourite and powerful openings.

Group and independent work

Read descriptive passages from other stories; list or highlight words and phrases that indicate setting; list unusual and/or interesting words.

Differentiation

Low Attainers – give the children a descriptive passage without illustration; ask them to draw a picture of the place described.

High Attainers – Copymaster 14: underline words that describe the setting; draw a picture of it.

Plenary

Ask one child or group to read their descriptive passage; ask the others to draw a quick sketch of the place they see in their mind's eye, and/or to jot down key words. Share responses orally; note similarities and differences. Share and discuss unusual and interesting words.

Lesson 4

Whole class

From descriptive passages read in previous lessons, select sentences that provide models for adaptation, *e.g. X lived in a tiny old cottage at the edge of the forest.* Write these up; talk through process of adaptation, using the first sentence as an example (Y lived in a big new house near the railway line). Then give the children time-out to write their own versions of this and the sentences. Encourage them to draw on the range of vocabulary introduced in the unit. Share and discuss contributions. Choose a place the children know well, *e.g. the local park or market, school-field or playground.* Give children, working in pairs, a few minutes to list words that could be used to describe this place. Support by focusing attention on different aspects, *e.g. what can be seen and heard.*

Record words as a concept map; look for opportunities to extend vocabulary by suggesting less familiar words. Use shared writing techniques to begin composing a description of the scene, drawing on this word bank.

Prompt children to distinguish between synonyms and to choose vivid, accurate words.

Group and independent work

Choose a place that they know well. List words that could be used to describe it; then write a description. Ask children to keep a note of descriptive words that they find difficult to spell.

Differentiation

Low Attainers – continue and develop the description begun in whole-class work.

High Attainers – encourage children to include vivid description of small details.

Plenary

Ask some children to read out their descriptions; ask others to comment, noting words that describe the place most vividly and clearly.

Share words that were difficult to spell. Identify similarities with other words; practise using 'look, say, cover, write, check'.

Lesson 5

Whole class

Remind children of the familiar place that they wrote a description of together in the previous lesson. Ask them: What characters might we meet here? What might happen? Share and jot down some ideas. Give children time-out to begin to develop a story-line.

Share ideas; choose one to develop as a story together. Discuss what the opening sentences of the story might be, drawing on possibilities identified and discussed in Lesson 3. Choose one that works best.

Use shared writing techniques to begin composing the story. Prompt children to include description of setting, drawing on the word bank compiled in the previous lesson.

As the writing proceeds, explain and demonstrate how to organise the text in paragraphs, e.g. an opening one setting the scene, the next introducing a character.

Group and independent work

Begin writing the story that might take place in the setting they chose in Lesson 4, incorporating all or some of this description. Encourage children to consider and choose between different story openings.

Differentiation

Low Attainers – write just the first episode of the story, focusing on description of setting.

High Attainers – develop a story with more than one setting.

Plenary

Share story openings. Which ones work well?

Read one or two first episodes; discuss how action, character and setting fit together.

Theme 8) Shape poems

Objectives

Text level:
- 8 express views about a poem
- 9 generate ideas relevant to a topic
- 12 collect suitable words and phrases to write poems; design simple patterns with words
- 13 invent calligrams and a range of shape poems

Word level:
- 8 understand how the spellings of verbs alters when *ing* is added
- 17 generate synonyms
- 19 recognise common vocabulary for introducing and concluding dialogue

Resources

A collection of calligrams and shape poems of different kinds; enlarged text versions of some of these. Copymasters 15 & 16. Homework 8.

Assessment

At the end of this theme is the pupil able to:
- share opinions about poems in discussion with others, explaining own views and referring to the text;
- choose words relevant to a particular topics, considering exact meanings carefully;
- experiment with words and layout to create shape poems and calligrams;
- use knowledge of patterns and rules to spell verbs ending in *ing*?

Lesson 1

Whole class

Draw on the board a large hand shape, showing fingers and thumb.
Along the length of one finger, write a verb ending with *ing* that describes something you do with your hands, *e.g. clapping, tying*. Ask the children to record things they enjoying doing with their hands in the same way on their whiteboards. Share and write up ideas. Choose four interesting, favourite words to write on the rest of the hand. Explain that together they have made a shape poem and that they will be reading and writing other kinds in the lessons that follow.
Repeat this process to create another poem which emphasises choice of vivid, powerful words, *e.g. hot-weather words displayed in the rays round a sun; swimming-pool words in splashes coming up from a dive.*
Return to the list of verbs ending in *ing*. Identify and explain spelling rules and patterns: doubling final consonant in verbs ending CVC (grab/grabbing); dropping final e in verbs ending VCV (dive/diving).

Group and independent work

Children write three verbs to illustrate the various spelling patterns. They then create their own shape poems, using ideas from whole-class work or inventing a similar idea of their own, and working on large sheets of paper.

Differentiation

Low Attainers – Copymaster 15: add *ing* to a list of verbs to do with moving fast; then use these words to make a shape poem, adding others of their own choice.
High Attainers – Copymaster 15: in addition, write rules to explain patterns for adding *ing*.

Plenary

Ask selected children to hold up and read their shape poems. Generate other words that could have been used.
Carry out a short spelling test focused on verbs ending in *ing*; mark; identify any difficulties, and revise teaching points.

Lesson 2

Whole class

Display a large text version of a shape poem in which words are used pictorially to make the shape of the subject. Identify the subject, and discuss how words are repeated and/or arranged to represent it.
Try to read the poem together. Identify any problems that this presents, *e.g. not knowing where to start, having to read from right to left or bottom to top.* Use to reinforce usual reading conventions and strategies.
Repeat with another shape poem of this kind.
Share ideas for another subject for a poem like this. Choose one likely to generate an interesting range of words, and with a simple shape, *e.g. tree, kite, ice-cream cone, guitar, yacht.* Give children, working in pairs, time-out to list words to do with this subject. Pool ideas and compile a list. Introduce or revise the term 'synonyms'; prompt the children to search their vocabularies to find examples of synonyms on this subject.

Sketch a large outline shape of the chosen object; experiment with arranging and repeating the selected words to fill or outline the shape.

Group and independent work

Children choose a subject of their own; list words to do with it, and use them to create a shape poem. This works well as a pair activity.

Differentiation

Low Attainers – use a word processor to create their poem (best with a straight-sided object).
High Attainers – use a thesaurus to help them compile a list of words.

Plenary

Display poems around the room, and give children a few minutes to look at and read them. Experiment with reading some out loud. Discuss the effect created.

Lesson 3

Whole class

Look at and discuss an enlarged text version of a shape poem in which words and/or letters are arranged to suggest an idea (see Copymaster 16 for an example). How does it work? Can you read it? Does it make you read in an unusual way?

Write up the word 'swoop'. Ask children to use their whiteboards to arrange and change the letters to make a one-word poem that suggests the meaning of the words *e.g. swoooooooop*, or arranging the letters to make the shallow v-shape of a bird in flight. Share ideas. Ask some children to write their poems on the board or a large sheet of paper. Try the same for other verbs, *e.g. climb, fall, explode*.

Write up words that represent more abstract ideas, feelings and situations, *e.g. disorganised, happy, broken, forgetful*. Use shared writing techniques to write sentences including them, *e.g. Mum is always saying how*

forgetful I am. Experiment with arranging the letters of the key word to suggest the idea it represents, *e.g. forgetfu (I forgot the L!)*.

Group and independent work

Children create shape poems of the two kinds explained and modelled in whole-class work, working with large sheets of unlined paper.

Differentiation

Low Attainers – offer children a list of suitable words for poems of these kinds.
High Attainers – Copymaster 16: read and answer questions about a shape poem. Write a longer shape poem, arranging words as well as letters.

Plenary

Display an enlarged text version of another shape poem of this kind. Prompt children to draw on their experience of writing similar poems to discuss how it works and to evaluate it.

Lesson 4

Whole class

Write up a few words used to introduce or conclude dialogue, *e.g. shout, whisper, mutter*. Rewrite 'shout' in big fat letters which suggest the volume of the utterance. Explain that this is a calligram, and is another way of using shape (and size) to represent the meaning of words. Use a mind-map to generate and record other words for dialogue; prompt children to search their vocabularies, and to identify and discuss the differences in meaning between synonyms, *e.g. shout, yell, bellow*. Give the children a few minutes to experiment with turning some of these words into calligrams, writing on small pieces of paper. Ask each child to choose his/her favourite calligram, and pin or stick them on a large sheet of paper to make a poem. Share ideas for titles. Decide which is best.

Write up a pair of opposite adjectives, *e.g. smooth, rough; tall, short*. Experiment with representing them as calligrams.

Group and independent work

Children list words that describe other actions, *e.g. ways of walking, moving, eating*; choose some to turn into calligrams that reflect their meanings.

Differentiation

Low Attainers – write calligrams for more pairs of opposite adjectives.
High Attainers – use calligrams in sentences to create a poem.

Plenary

Share words for one of the categories of action; add new ones, and discuss exact meanings.
Create and title a group poem consisting of calligrams on the same subject; choose a title for it.

Lesson 5

Whole class

Display around the room the shape poems and calligrams that the class have written. Ask the children to look at and read them, and to choose a favourite. After a few minutes, gather the children together, and choose some to share their favourites with the class. Prompt them to say just what they like and to explain their reasons. Encourage the other children to contribute their own ideas about each of these poems. Organise this so that different kinds of poems are represented, and continue until five or six have been discussed.

Ask children to imagine that they are the editors of an anthology of shape poems and calligrams. Share ideas about how the poems in the anthology might be organised and whether there should be illustrations. Explain that shape poems are very rarely illustrated, and discuss why this should be.

Group and independent work

Children work in groups of five or six, sharing the poems they have written and choosing – say – 12 for an anthology. You could make it a rule that each child should have one of his/her poems included. Each child then makes a new, carefully presented copy of his/her poem(s). Collectively the groups decide how to organise the poems.

Differentiation

Low Attainers – compile, organise and present an anthology consisting of one poem by each child in the group.
High Attainers – in addition, write a short introduction for their anthology.

Plenary

Ask groups to present their selections, explaining how they chose and organised the poems.
Plan and organise the work to create group anthologies 'published' to a standard for other classes to read.

Theme 9) Synonyms and thesauruses

Objectives

Text level:
- 9 generate words relevant to a topic

Sentence level:
- 3 investigate function of verbs in sentences, through experimenting with changing verbs

Word level:
- 6 use independent spelling strategies
- 7 practise new spellings
- 16 understand the purpose and organisation of the thesaurus, and use it to find synonyms
- 17 generate synonyms for high-frequency words
- 18 use the term 'synonym'

Resources

A set of simple thesauruses (at least enough for one between two or three children); enlarged text pages or extracts from this. Other thesauruses organised in different ways, if these are in use in the school. Enlarged text extract from a novel, including adventurous vocabulary choices and words likely to be unfamiliar.
Enlarged text with dull, repetitive use of words, especially adjectives.
Copymasters 17 & 18. Homework 9.

Assessment

At the end of this theme is the pupil able to:
- use a simple thesaurus to aid word choice;
- generate and choose between synonyms;
- make a text more interesting by improving choice of words;
- use a range of spelling strategies to attempt new words?

Lesson 1

Whole class

Explain that this unit is about choosing words, and about a reference text that helps with this. Introduce the term 'thesaurus'.
Prepare by covering unfamiliar and/or powerful words in the enlarged text story extract. Read this with the children. When you reach the first hidden word, prompt them to speculate about what it might be. Discuss possibilities, re-reading the sentence with these inserted. Reveal and discuss the word in the text.
Read the rest of the text together. At each hidden word, give children, working in pairs, a brief time-out to list possibilities. Encourage them to have a try at spelling new words. Share, try out and discuss ideas, and reveal the actual word, as above.
When less familiar words are suggested, prompt children to work out spellings, recording attempts on the board. Look for opportunities to develop spelling strategies and extend knowledge of spelling patterns.

Group and independent work

Give children cloze texts similar to that used in whole-class work, with selected verbs, adjectives and adverbs blanked out. When individuals have filled in the gaps, share and discuss choices with others in their group.

Differentiation

Low Attainers – recreate the text read in whole class work, extending it by a few sentences.
High Attainers – write a list of alternatives for words (verbs, adjectives and adverbs) underlined in a text.

Plenary

Ask children to share different possibilities for filling a gap in a text. Discuss together, and try to reach agreement on the best choice.
Monitor work to select less familiar words; try out strategies for spelling them.

Lesson 2

Whole class

Read together the enlarged text with obviously exaggeratedly boring, repetitive vocabulary. Ask children what they notice. Work together to replace the first such word, compiling a list of possibilities with similar meanings. Introduce the term 'synonym' for words like this. Discuss and try out alternatives as in Lesson 1, make a choice, and write the word in.
For each of the remaining 'dull' words, ask individual children to write a few possibilities, and then share them with a partner. Share words as a class, discuss differences in meaning, and choose one to write in.
Write up a list of high frequency words for which there is a range of synonyms (see Copymaster 18 for possibilities). Ask children to work in pairs to write a list of these, then share as a class. As before discuss differences in meaning.
Work together on spelling strategies for selected new words, *e.g. ones which provide opportunities for revising spelling patterns children are unsure of.*

Group and independent work

Write up four more high frequency words, and ask children to list three synonyms for each. Give them a subject, *e.g. school dinners, going swimming,* and challenge them to write a few sentences about it, choosing interesting words.

Differentiation

Low Attainers – Copymaster 17: replace 'dull' words in another text.
High Attainers – Copymaster 18: list synonyms for given high-frequency words.

Plenary

Share 'interesting' sentences; discuss word choices, considering possible alternatives.
Pool contributions to compile a class list of synonyms for high frequency words.

Lesson 3
Whole class

Introduce the thesaurus, explaining its function in relation to work in Lessons 1 and 2, that is, to choose more varied and interesting words.

Distribute copies of the class thesaurus to pairs to look at and read. Ask the children what they notice. Use their comments as the basis for explaining how words are selected and organised, illustrating this with reference to particular pages. Emphasise the idea that the book lists synonyms.

If the thesaurus is organised alphabetically, explain the selection of 'key words' and any index; if thematically, explain what the categories are and how they are arranged.

Return to the 'dull' text used in Lesson 2. Model the process of looking up the first 'dull' word. Look at the list of synonyms, identifying any that they did not think of themselves.

Circle other 'dull' words and assign to pairs of children to look up. Share results.

Group and independent work
Assign to groups one or two of the high frequency words; look them up in the thesaurus; and add any new synonyms to the list compiled at the end of Lesson 2. Give children (or write up) a text with, say, five underlined words for them to look up and replace.

Differentiation
Low Attainers – use a thesaurus to write their own version of the 'dull' text from Lesson 2.
High Attainers – find in the thesaurus the adventurous and less familiar words in the text read in Lesson 1; replace with synonyms.

Plenary
Share new synonyms for high frequency words. Share and discuss the meaning of words to replace underlined words in the text.

Lesson 4
Whole class

Identify and highlight the verbs in an enlarged text; ask the children to use their thesauruses to suggest alternatives. Re-read sentences with these substitutions, and discuss changes in effect.

Write up a few adjectives and briefly revise the word 'adjective'. Ask children to work in pairs to list an adjective related to each of the senses except smell, *e.g. bright, loud, hard*, and to use their thesauruses to compile a list of synonyms. Share new and interesting words. Suggest nouns for children to look up, *e.g. fight, house, piece, pile, story*. Share and discuss words found; point out that synonyms here often refer to a particular type within a broad category.

During the course of this work, look for opportunities to explain how (in alphabetical thesauruses) entries for many key words are organised in areas of meaning –

e.g. the entry for 'hard' will include words related to 'difficulty' as well as to touch.

Group and independent work
Provide a text (or texts at various levels of challenge) and ask children to use their thesaurus to experiment with changing three verbs, three adjectives and three nouns.

Differentiation
Low Attainers – underline appropriate words for changing; and/or focus only on adjectives.
High Attainers – work with a text including dialogue introduced with 'said'; rewrite using alternative verbs.

Plenary
Read through an enlarged version of one of the texts used, pausing for children to say where and how they changed words.

Ask children to look up words that require them to use the index and/or to find the right area of meaning. Model the processes involved.

Lesson 5
Whole class

Choose a subject for writing about which provides potential for using a wide range of adjectives and verbs, *e.g. an animal, a machine*.

Ask children to suggest words that could be used to describe this subject, and record them using a mind-map to record and sort the words, *e.g. words for movement, appearance, touch.* Identify any sets of synonyms that occur, *e.g. by highlighting or underlining in a different colour.*

Give children time-out to use their thesauruses to find alternatives for two of these words. Share words, and add to the mind-map.

Draw on this word bank to write interesting sentences, using shared writing techniques. Encourage children to find the precise and vivid word.

As new words are suggested, model use of spelling strategies to attempt them; confirm correct spelling.

Group and independent work
Children choose a subject of their own; generate a bank of words to describe it, unaided to start with, then using a thesaurus to extend the range. Draw on this to write a vivid description. Towards the end of this phase, ask children to choose their best sentence.

Differentiation
Low Attainers – write their own description of the subject used in whole-class work.
High Attainers – challenge children to write sentences which include one vivid verb and two vivid adjectives.

Plenary
Ask children to read their 'best' sentences'; ask others to comment on the word choice.
Choose some unfamiliar words and work together to spell them.

Theme 10 Verbs

Objectives

Sentence level:
- 1 use awareness of grammar to decipher new or unfamiliar words
- 3 investigate the function of verbs in sentences
- 4 use verb tenses with increasing accuracy; use past tense consistently for narration
- 5 use the term 'verb'

Word level:
- 8 know how the spelling of verbs alters when *ing* is added
- 9 investigate and learn to use the spelling pattern *le*
- 17 generate synonyms for high frequency words
- 19 recognise a common vocabulary for introducing and concluding dialogue

Resources
An enlarged text extract from a past tense narrative.
An enlarged narrative text with 'deliberate mistakes' in verb use, including: non-standard forms, *e.g. tooked;* irregular past tense forms, *e.g. caught, wrote;* inconsistencies of tense, especially slipping from past into present (see Copymaster 20 for examples). Cards with verbs (in the infinitive form) making five or six sets of synonyms *e.g. for look or run.* Differentiated cloze procedure texts with verbs deleted.
Copymasters 19 & 20. Homework 10.

Assessment
At the end of this theme is the pupil able to:
- identify verbs in sentences and explain their function;
- change verbs in sentences, and discuss the effect on meaning;
- generate and distinguish between verb synonyms;
- use past tense verbs accurately and consistently in narrative writing;
- understand spelling rules related to the addition of *ing* to the verb root?

Lesson 1

Whole class

Prepare for this lesson by concealing all or most of the verbs in an enlarged text extract from a story. Read through the text together, pausing for children to work out the hidden word while drawing on grammatical and contextual information. Underline each verb as it is revealed.

When all the words have been revealed, ask children what they notice; guide children to the idea that they all have the same function: to indicate actions or states of being. Introduce the term 'verb' and explain that in the following lessons they will be learning more about these words. Cover up some of the verbs again; read the sentence without them; explain that the sentence does not make sense without this word. (Contrast where possible with deleting adjectives or adverbs which do not (generally) destroy meaning).

Give each child a verb card and the task of composing (orally or on paper) a sentence including this verb. Share contributions, and write some down. Identify and underline the verb.

Group and independent work
Children identify, by listing or underlining, the verbs in a short text (these could be differentiated according to reading ability), stopping when they have found five. Write another sentence using each of these verbs.

Differentiation
Low Attainers – give each child five verb cards and the challenge of writing a sentence including each.
High Attainers – in addition, ask children to write sentences for each of five verbs of their own choice.

Plenary
Choose children to read one of the sentences they have written; ask others to put their hands up when they hear the verb. Write up a list of these verbs.

Lesson 2

Whole class

Return to the narrative text from Lesson 1. Focus on the first verb (ignoring for this purpose the verb 'to be').
Ask the children to suggest another verb that could take its place. List possibilities; read the sentences that result, and discuss changes in meaning and effect.
Give pairs time-out to find alternatives for the next two or three verbs. Share, discuss and try out possibilities. Identify and list the verbs used to set up dialogue; ask children to write five more; compile a class list. Choose some; ask children to say something to their partners in that 'tone of voice'.
Give out the verb cards again; ask children to organise themselves into word 'families'. Share the resulting sets of synonyms. Choose one group; work together to compose, orally, a sentence including each of the verbs.

Group and independent work
Individual children fill gaps in cloze texts with verbs deleted. Give each group a verb with a broad meaning, *e.g. walk, eat, talk, throw, break,* and ask them to work together to generate a list of verbs with similar meanings.

Differentiation
Low Attainers – Copymaster 19: choose verbs to fill gaps in sentences.
High Attainers – Copymaster 19: in addition, use each of the verb synonyms in a sentence which illustrates its meaning.

Plenary
Ask children who worked on the same cloze text to read it, presenting the different verbs they chose for each gap; discuss the effect of different choices.
Ask children who listed verb synonyms to 'perform' each action; ask others if they can guess the word. Discuss differences in meaning.

Lesson 3

Whole class

Write up sentences (from Lesson 2) with verbs ending in *ing* and *ed*. Identify the verbs, and ask children what they notice. Draw out the idea that the form of the verb changes. Highlight the ending, drawing a vertical line between this and the root word.

Distribute the verb cards, and ask children to compose a sentence using their verb. Share contributions; identify how the verb has been changed; and list examples ending in *ing*.

Use this list (adding more words as necessary) to illustrate related spelling rules: doubling final consonant in words ending CVC; dropping the final e. Write up examples of verbs which follow each rule; ask children to add *ing*; confirm correct spelling.

Say a word that ends with the letter string *le*, e.g. *grumble, wiggle, fizzle*. Ask who knows how to spell it.

Use attempts to explain the pattern. Work together to generate and spell similar words.

Group and independent work

Write up verbs (in the infinitive) which illustrate the patterns for adding *ing*; ask children to write sentences including the verb with this ending.

Write up words ending in *le*; ask children to write rhyming words.

Differentiation

Low Attainers – prepare a simple cloze text with gaps for verbs ending with *ing*.

High Attainers – write as many verbs ending with *le* as they can, sorting them into rhyming sets; use five in sentences where they need an *ing* ending.

Plenary

Carry out a spelling test with *ing* verbs, including some ending with *le*; check answers; revise rules as appropriate.

Lesson 4

Whole class

Display the narrative text with deliberate mistakes. Read it together until you reach the first error. *Ask: Is that right?* Prompt children to identify and correct the error. Ask them to read on independently, identifying errors and writing the correct word. Differentiate this by asking children to read sentences in which the error is more or less obvious.

Work through the text together, confirming each error; identifying the nature of the problem; and writing the correct word.

Write up sentences with gaps to be filled by verbs in the correct standard form and with simple irregular past tense forms, *e.g. X (came) first in the race.* Ask children to write down the verb that fits; check answers. Practise spellings as appropriate.

Use shared writing techniques to continue the narrative; focus on using verbs in the past tense.

Group and independent work

Children write three more sentences to continue the story, underlining the verbs.

Write up the sentence beginning 'Yesterday I ...' and a list of appropriate verbs, including some which are irregular in the past tense. Ask children to use them to complete the sentence.

Differentiation

Low Attainers – prepare a cloze activity with past tense verbs deleted.

High Attainers – Copymaster 20: find and correct errors of verb use in a narrative text.

Plenary

Choose a story continuation; read it to the class; pause at each verb for them to suggest possibilities; check their use of past tense.

Ask children to share 'Yesterday I ...' sentences with irregular verbs; check for correct form and spelling.

Lesson 5

Whole class

Set up contexts for shared writing in different tenses. Share facts about an animal; use them as the basis for writing a short non-chronological report in the simple present tense, *e.g. Cats sleep a lot.*

Share experiences about their first day at school, and record them in the past tense. Look for opportunities to revise spelling rules for adding *ed* and irregular standard past tense forms, *e.g. caught, not catched.*

Ask children what they are going to do sometime in the near future. Write sentences using different verb forms to express future actions, *e.g. I will ...; I am going to ...* Revise spelling rules for adding *ing*.

In each case, underline the verbs used, and explain and demonstrate consistency of tense, e.g. by making

deliberate mistakes. Once the tense has been established, give children time-out to compose sentences.

Group and independent work

Children write three sentences about each of the contexts used in whole-class work, but choosing a new animal for the first. Ask them to underline the verbs.

Differentiation

Low Attainers – give children sentence starters, e.g. *Elephants ...; On my first day at school I ...*

High Attainers – write more extended and coherent texts for each context.

Plenary

Use shared writing techniques to compose sentences in the past tense about what they have just done and learned; identify verbs; check tense and spellings.

Theme 1) Characters

Objectives

Text level:
- 3 identify and discuss main and recurring characters; evaluate their behaviour
- 6 plan main points as a structure for story writing
- 8 write portraits of characters

Sentence level:
- 2 investigate the function of adjectives in sentences (identify; collect and classify)
- 3 use the term 'adjective'
- 8 understand the use of capitalisation for names

Word level:
- 13 recognise and spell common suffixes
- 14 use knowledge of suffixes to generate new words
- 15 use the apostrophe to spell shortened forms of words
- 16 use the term 'suffix'

Resources

A 'core' story which features a clear main character and in which behaviour and motivation are important. Enlarged text extracts from this story – one of which includes dialogue. A collection of other stories in which character is a significant element. Cards with matching full and shortened forms, *e.g. do not/don't*.

NOTE: Prepare for this unit by asking children to choose a favourite story; guide them to one in which character is important and there are passages of dialogue. Copymasters 21 & 22. Homework 11.

Assessment

At the end of this theme is the pupil able to:
- identify the main character in a story and comment on his/her behaviour;
- represent and respond to character in a variety of ways;
- choose and use adjectives to describe aspects of a character;
- plan and write a story episode in which character is highlighted;
- begin names with a capital letter;
- spell shortened forms of words, placing apostrophes accurately;
- identify, read and spell words ending with common suffixes?

Lesson 1

Whole class

Explain that in this lesson they will be exploring characters in stories. Read the 'core' story to the children. Prompt children to identify the main and other characters in the story, and write up their names. Explain and demonstrate the use of capital letters at the start of names. Choose an extract from the story in which the focus is on the behaviour of the main character. Help children to recall events up to this point. Read the enlarged text together.

Prompt them to discuss what the character does and why. Use this as the starting point for a discussion of his/her personality and behaviour. Ask children to imagine that this character is a real person and that they are going to write a letter to him/her. What would they say? Focus on offering the character advice related to the predicament on which the story is based. Quickly revise letter conventions, and give pairs time-out to compose the first sentence or two, orally or on their whiteboards. Share ideas, relating them to the story, and use shared writing techniques to draft the letter.

Group and independent work

Children list main and other characters in their chosen story, and write a letter offering the main character advice.

Differentiation

Low Attainers – give children sentence-starters for their letter, e.g. *I think you are ...; I think you should ...*
High Attainers – ask children to develop points in their letter, relating them to the detail of the story.

Plenary

Ask children to name the main characters in their stories; write up these names, making deliberate errors in capitalisation.
Choose children to read their letters. Ask others to comment on the advice offered.

Lesson 2

Whole class

Write up the words 'short', 'long', 'curly' Ask children to put up their hands to show which of these words describes their hair. Introduce the term 'adjective' and describe its function.

Read together an enlarged text extract or extracts from the core story in which the main character is described. Identify the adjectives. Give children time-out to record other adjectives that could be used to describe this character. Compile a list.

Focus on adjectives ending with suffixes, *e.g. helpful, careless*, adding examples. Ask children what they notice about these words. Draw out the idea that a 'part' is added on at the end. Introduce the term 'suffix'. Generate other adjectives ending with these suffixes.

Group and independent work

Write up a list of appropriate root words, and ask children to create new words by adding the suffix *ful* or *less* (and/or prepare this as a worksheet).
Generate a list of adjectives to describe aspects of the main character in their chosen story.

Differentiation

Low Attainers – Copymaster 21: complete sentences by adding an adjective ending with *less* or 'ful'.
High Attainers – Copymaster 21: adjectives that end with these suffixes and which describe their character.

Plenary

Share adjectives ending with suffixes *ful* and *less*. Distinguish between spelling of the suffix *ful* and the word 'full'.
Classify adjectives to compile lists for aspects of appearance and personality.

Lesson 3

Whole class

Return to the list of main and other characters from Lesson 1. Draw lines between the characters, and prompt children to identify the relationships between them. Write words that describe this, *e.g. friends, father and son, along the lines.*

Ask children to imagine that the main character in the story gets lost, and that they have to write a 'missing persons' poster. Explain that they are going to start by describing his/her appearance. Ask children to write a sentence about this. Display the list of adjectives from Lesson 2 for them to refer to. Share contributions, and compose a joint text.

Next prompt children to suggest where the character might be and what he/she might be doing. Use shared writing techniques to write sentences about this.

Group and independent work

Add relationship lines to the list of characters they wrote in Lesson 1.

Design and write a missing persons poster for the main character in their chosen story, drawing on the adjectives they listed in Lesson 2. Work on large sheet of paper.

Differentiation

Low Attainers – draw a picture of the character and label it to give more information.

High Attainers – write a missing persons report in which there is no help from a picture.

Plenary

Display the posters round the room and give children a few minutes to look at and read some of them. Discuss which are the most clear and helpful, and why.

Lesson 4

Whole class

Read together an extract from the 'core' story in which the main character is in conversation with another character or characters. Re-read, organising children to take 'parts'. Prompt them to discuss what can be learned about the character and his/her relationships with other people by what he/she says and how it is said.

Revise (from Autumn Term) the layout and punctuation of dialogue.

Ask children to imagine that they are involved in this scene: What would they say to the main character? What would he/she say to them? Ask pairs to write a short exchange of dialogue, using speech bubbles or speech marks.

Highlight shortened forms of words in the dialogue, and ask children what they notice about them. Explain how two words are joined together and that the apostrophe shows where letters have been missed out.

Distribute full and short form cards, and ask children to find the matching pairs. Choose children to present the words joined and the letter(s) omitted.

Group and independent work

Children work with Copymaster 22 to complete pairs of short and full forms.

Ask children to write a short dialogue between the main character in their chosen story and themselves (with a partner).

Differentiation

Low Attainers – work only with short forms including 'not'.

High Attainers – include short forms in their dialogue, and use speech marks.

Plenary

Choose children to perform the dialogues they have written with a partner.

Write up and explain more complex shortened forms, *e.g. won't, I'll.*

Lesson 5

Whole class

Draw together ideas about the 'core' story, and explain that they are going to introduce a new character into it. Share ideas about who this could be; encourage children to stay within the 'world' of the story. Agree on a new character.

Organise the class into four groups, and ask each to develop one aspect of this new character: personality and relationships, appearance, clothes, interests. Ask them to record this by listing adjectives (as in Lesson 2) or writing a descriptive sentence or sentences (as in Lesson 3). Designate one child in each group to act as scribe.

Ask each group to present their ideas, and compose a joint portrait of the character.

Choose an episode from the story, and introduce the new character into it. Ask: *What would the new character and the main character say to each other? What would they*

do? Use shared writing techniques to draft a short episode, including some dialogue.

Group and independent work

Children create a new character for their chosen story, describing him/her by listing adjectives or writing descriptive sentences. They then choose an episode in the story and write a short dialogue between this character and the main character.

Differentiation

Low Attainers – draw and label a picture of their new character, and write an exchange of dialogue in speech bubbles.

High Attainers – write a new episode featuring this character, including narrative and dialogue.

Plenary

Choose children to tell the class about their new character, and to read the dialogue or episode they have written. Look out for opportunities to revisit teaching points about aspects of character and adjectives.

Theme 2) Dictionaries

Objectives

Word level:
- 5 identify misspelt words
- 6 use independent spelling strategies
- 10 investigate, spell and read words with silent letters
- 13 recognise and spell words ending with common suffixes
- 18 infer the meaning of unknown words from context
- 19 use dictionaries to learn or check the spellings and definitions of words
- 20 write own definitions of words, developing precision and accuracy
- 21 use the term 'definition'
- 22 know the quartiles of the dictionary
- 23 organise words alphabetically, using the first two letters

Resources

Copies of the main class dictionary. A range of other dictionaries. An alphabet frieze or chart. For Lesson 2, pictures illustrating words which include silent letters. For Lesson 4, an enlarged text containing misspellings illustrating different kinds of errors, including ones related to content of Lesson 2 (silent letters) and Lesson 3 (rules for adding suffixes *er*, *est* and *ly*). For Lesson 5, an enlarged text including some words that are likely to be new to the children.
Copymasters 23 & 24. Homework 12.

Assessment

At the end of this theme is the pupil able to:
- identify misspelt words, using a range of strategies for checking;
- use a range of strategies to attempt new spellings;
- work with a dictionary efficiently, using knowledge of relative positions of letters in the alphabet;
- use dictionaries to check spellings and the meanings of words;
- write clear and accurate definitions of words;
- search alphabetical lists of words beginning with the same letter;
- spell words ending with common suffixes, and find them in a dictionary?

Lesson 1

Whole class

Explain that in this unit they will be learning more about using dictionaries. Display the alphabet frieze.
Say a word, identify the initial letter, and ask: *Where will you find this word in the dictionary? Near the beginning? Around the middle? Near the end?* Check the position of the letter on the frieze. Repeat.
Distribute the dictionaries. Ask children to open the dictionary at a given word. How close did they get? Repeat with other words.
Write up a list of words with the same initial letter but each with different second letters. Explain how these are arranged in alphabetical order. Sort the first two or three together, then give the children time-out to list the rest. Check.
Ask children to open their dictionaries at the beginning of a section, and say words beginning with that letter for them to find. Relate this to relative positions: words beginning *sa* will be near the beginning, words beginning with *sw* near the end.

Group and independent work

Prepare worksheets, or display lists of words for children to sort by second letter.
Play 'opening the dictionary' as a game: who gets the right letter?

Differentiation

Low Attainers – Copymaster 23: decide whether to go backwards or forwards in the dictionary to find a given word.
High Attainers – play 'opening the dictionary' within one (large) section, e.g. B, C, S.

Plenary

Ask a child to try to open the dictionary at a given word; the child says the letter he or she has found; ask others whether forwards or backwards is the right direction.
Say a word; see who can find it in the dictionary first.

Lesson 2

Whole class

Write up and read the word 'knee'. Ask children what the problem might be when looking for it in the dictionary. Explain that in this word *k* is a 'silent' letter. Ask pairs of children to write a list of other words beginning like this. Share and confirm. Use the 'look, say, cover, write, check' method to practise these spellings. Repeat for words beginning *gn*.
Explain that silent letters also come in the middle of words. Ask them to try spelling words such as walk, listen, sign. Share and confirm spellings, highlighting the letter that is not sounded. Practise as before.
Repeat this teaching sequence for words ending with silent letters, *e.g. comb, hymn*.

Group and independent work

Children write lists of words beginning with *wr* and with silent *l* in the middle.
Then draw on and extend whole-class work to compile an alphabetical list of words beginning with silent letters, looking in the dictionary to find other examples.

Differentiation

Low Attainers – label pictures of things including silent letters; circle the silent letter.
High Attainers – compile organised lists of words with silent letters in the middle or at the end.

Plenary

Pool and write up words starting with *wr* and including silent *l* in the middle.
Ask children to contribute words with silent letters not discussed in whole-class work. Write up; highlight silent letter. Find others with the same pattern.

Lesson 3

Whole class

Write up the word 'bigger' and ask children to look for it in the dictionary. Report back. Explain that some words do not have entries of their own but are listed with the main word (or headword). Repeat with words ending with other common suffixes, *e.g. gently, helpless, useful.* Together, read the entry for one of these headwords; explain how derived words are organised. Ask children what they notice about the spelling of the word 'bigger'. Explain the rule for doubling the final consonant in words ending CVC. Write up similar words, *e.g. thin, sad,* and ask children to write sets of words ending with *er* and *est.* Share and confirm spellings.

Write up the word 'dirty', and ask children to add *er* and *est.* Explain the rule for dropping the final *e,* and demonstrate and practise with other examples.

Repeat this sequence to explain and practise rules for adding *ly* to words ending with *e* (gently) and *y* (luckily).

Group and independent work

Write up a list of words ending with common suffixes; ask children to write the headword they would need to find in the dictionary.

Write a list of adjectives which demonstrate the various rules, and ask children to add *er, est* and *ly.* You could present this as worksheets.

Differentiation

Low Attainers – concentrate on doubling/not doubling the final consonant.

High Attainers – write an explanation of the rules.

Plenary

Say other words with suffixes; ask children to identify the headword under which it would be listed.

Share and confirm spellings of words which demonstrate the spelling rules covered.

Lesson 4

Whole class

Distribute the dictionaries and display the enlarged text with deliberate misspellings. Read it together, prompting children to spot and correct the first error. Ask them to identify and explain the problem.

Explain that dictionaries are used to find or check the spelling of a word; explain and demonstrate for the word in question.

Give pairs of children time-out to identify and correct the other spelling mistakes. Then work through the text line by line, prompting children to explain the nature of each error. Reinforce knowledge of relevant spelling rules and patterns. Confirm the correct spelling. Check some words in the dictionary.

Say a sentence which includes one word that is tricky to spell, *e.g. pigeon, castle, photograph, because.* Prompt children to identify this word, and to have a go at

spelling it. Work together to use a range of strategies to attempt its spelling. Confirm the correct spelling by finding the word in the dictionary.

Group and independent work

Ask children to look back at a recent piece (or pieces) of writing, and identify and list five words that they have misspelt. Attempt to correct them; then look up the word in the dictionary to check, and write the correct spelling if necessary.

Differentiation

Low Attainers – 'mark' a piece of writing, identifying misspellings to work on.

High Attainers – Copymaster 24: correct spelling errors.

Plenary

Introduce or develop a routine in which children keep individual lists of words that they need to practise spelling.

Lesson 5

Whole class

Read together the text with unfamiliar and unusual words. Pause at the first such word, and prompt children to infer its meaning from the context. Generate and record a list of possible meanings or areas of meaning, *e.g. it could be some kind of colour.* Explain that another use of dictionaries is to find or check the meaning of unfamiliar words. Ask children working in pairs to look up the word in question. Confirm its meaning. Read the definition together, and introduce this term.

Read the rest of the text, following this procedure for some or all of the remaining 'new' words.

Discuss the style of the definitions (as used in the class dictionary); emphasise the importance of accuracy and precision.

List interesting and/or special words to do with school life, *e.g. assembly, sin-bin, bean-bag.* Choose one, and ask children to write a definition. Share contributions, and

discuss their accuracy and precision. Use shared writing techniques to compose a joint definition. Repeat for some of the other school words.

Group and independent work

Children write their own definitions for five special words to do with a subject that they are interested in.

Differentiation

Low Attainers – write definitions for given words, providing the opening to establish the style.

High Attainers – follow the layout and language conventions of the class dictionary.

Plenary

Choose children to read out a definition without revealing the word; ask others to guess what this is. Revise some definitions to make them more clear and useful.

Read out definitions from the class dictionary and ask children what the word is.

Theme 3) Fables

Objectives

Text level:
- 1 investigate the styles and voices of traditional story language
- 2 identify story themes
- 3 identify and discuss main and recurring characters
- 6 plan main points as a structure for story writing
- • describe and sequence key incidents in a variety of ways
- 9 write a story-plan for own fable

Sentence level:
- 2 investigate the function of adjectives within sentences
- 3 use the term 'adjective' appropriately
  Revise from Autumn Term: using punctuation as a guide for reading; writing in and demarcating sentences

Word level:
- 8 how words change when er, est and y are added
- 13 recognise and spell common suffixes
- 24 explore opposites

Resources
Collections and photocopies of fables written at different levels of difficulty, e.g. The Best of Aesop's Fables, retold by Margaret Clark, illustrated by Charlotte Voake (Walker Books); and the more challenging Aesop's Fables, retold by Anne Gatti, illustrated by Safaya Salter (Pavilion Books).
Enlarged text version of two fables to work with as 'core' texts, e.g. Fables (Rigby).
Copymasters 25 & 26. Homework 13.

Assessment
At the end of this theme is the pupil able to:
- identify and discuss the characteristic thematic and language features of fables;
- use a variety of techniques to chart key events in a story;
- identify and discuss the use of adjectives in a text;
- collect adjectives and use them in their own writing;
- recognise common suffixes and understand how they change the meaning of the root word;
- understand spelling rules related to adding common suffixes;
- plan and write own fable, drawing on themes and characters from reading?

Lesson 1

Whole class

Read the first fable to the children while they follow the text. Give pairs of children time-out to share ideas about it, and then discuss as a class.
Re-read the text together; draw children's attention to punctuation and prompt them to use it as a guide to phrasing and intonation. Re-read sentences to make the sense clearer.
Ask pairs to record the key events in the story in list form on their whiteboards. Share and compare work. Identify and discuss the characters in the story. Ask children to list any adjectives used to describe them; highlight these in the text. Describe and discuss the characters' 'personalities' and their roles in the story. Prompt children to identify the main idea or 'moral' of the story. Introduce the term 'fable' and explain the characteristics of this kind of traditional story.

Group and independent work
Read other fables (differentiated for reading level), and use Copymaster 25 to analyse and record key elements, related to whole-class work. Plan and rehearse a read-aloud performance of the fable.

Differentiation
Low Attainers – re-read and complete Copymaster 25 for the fable read in the whole-class phase.
High Attainers – Copymaster 25: in addition list all the adjectives used in their fable.

Plenary
Draw up a class list of characters in the fables that were read. Ask children to explain the 'moral' that their fable illustrates; write a list.
Choose children to read their fable to the class; invite sensitive comments on clarity.

Lesson 2

Whole class

Return to the list of animal characters compiled in Lesson 1. Choose one that features frequently in fables and other traditional stories, e.g. wolf or fox. Prompt children to think about how this animal is depicted, and to write words to describe it.
Share and write up these words. Identify the adjectives. Use shared writing techniques to compose sentences about the animal including the adjectives, e.g. The cunning fox . . .
Highlight adjectives ending in the suffix y or ful, adding other examples if necessary. Explain and demonstrate related spelling rules. Ask children to write words with these endings. Check spellings.
Ask children how this animal would perform a particular action, e.g. walking, eating, talking. Highlight use of adverbs to describe this, e.g. slowly, greedily, gently. Identify the ly suffix, and explain and demonstrate related spelling rules.

Group and independent work
Ask children to choose an animal, and to list words that could be used to describe its appearance, its personality in stories and how it behaves.

Differentiation
Low Attainers – Copymaster 26: choose adjectives to use in sentences about animals; add ly to change adjectives into adverbs.
High Attainers – go on to write a short description of the animal, drawing on their word-bank.

Plenary
Pool words; sort into sets those which end in suffixes y, ful, less and ly. Reinforce spelling rules focusing on how the spelling of the root word changes in some cases.

Lesson 3

Whole class

Prepare for this lesson by compiling a list of words in this and the first fable that have opposites.

Display the enlarged text version of the second fable; choose children to read a sentence or two each to the class. Re-read selected sentences, explaining how the punctuation helps readers to 'make sense'. Re-read the whole fable together.

Develop the work in Lesson 1 by giving children time-out in pairs to:
• record the key events in sequence as a numbered list;
• list the characters and words used to describe them and how they behave;
• identify the moral and state it in one sentence;
• share ideas. Look for opportunities to differentiate between key events and ones of lesser importance;
• identify adjectives and adverbs, suffixes, and related spelling rules;
• organise ideas in a single clear sentence.

Display the list of words with opposites. Find the opposite of the first one together; then ask children to write others. Share and confirm.

Group and independent work

Read another fable, and use Copymaster 25 again to record key elements. Re-read the two fables they have read independently; list words that have opposites, and complete the pairs.

Differentiation

Low Attainers – give children a list of common opposite pairs to complete.
High Attainers – in addition, write a short comparison of the two fables.

Plenary

Share pairs of opposite words; check by discussing the question: Are these real opposites?
Prompt children to identify and discuss similarities and differences between the four fables they have read.

Lesson 4

Whole class

Explain that in this lesson they will be planning two new fables.

1) Together, choose a moral from one of the fables read; write it up. Ask children to work with a partner to work out a new story to illustrate this moral. Who will be in the story? What will happen? Share ideas, and choose one to develop together. Use shared writing techniques to plan the main events, using a story ladder.

2) Brainstorm and record other 'morals' or guides to behaviour, *e.g. ones related to school life (Share the pencil sharpener; Never run in the corridor)*. Choose one to use as the basis for a fable. Give pairs of children time-out to work out a story-line, deciding on characters and plot. Share and discuss ideas focusing in particular on the appropriateness of the animal characters. Choose a

story-line to develop together, and plan the main events using a different technique, *e.g. a simple storyboard*.

Group and independent work

Children plan a new fable of their own, drawing on examples they have read and the two possibilities modelled in whole-class work. Work on large sheets of paper, using one of the planning techniques demonstrated.

Differentiation

Low Attainers – plan a new fable to illustrate the moral from a familiar fable, using picture planning.
High Attainers – plan a fable to illustrate a new modern, relevant moral.

Plenary

Share and discuss some plans. Prompt children to draw on their knowledge of the characteristic features of fables to comment and to suggest improvements.

Lesson 5

Whole class

Choose one of the fables planned together in the previous lesson. Generate and record adjectives that could be used to describe the characters, *e.g. using mind-maps*.

Ask pairs of children to think about how the fable might begin and to write the first two sentences. Share story openings. Are they right for a fable? Which ones work well? Choose some to write up and develop. Revise organisation of ideas in short, simple sentences and demarcation with capital letters and full stops.

Move on to a part of the story where dialogue could feature. Ask pairs of children to role-play what the characters might say, and to write a short exchange of dialogue. Share these; demonstrate how to record dialogue using speech bubbles and speech marks.

Group and independent work

Children write the fable which they planned in Lesson 4. Though short, this task offers an opportunity for more extended writing across subsequent Literacy Hours and/or outside this context, and for revision and presentation for others to read.

Differentiation

Low Attainers – add narrative captions and speech bubbles to their picture-plan to produce a fable in strip cartoon form.
High Attainers – encourage children to use the language features of fables read.

Plenary

Share and discuss work in progress; prompt children to identify and discuss the strengths and points for improvement.
Plan a class book of fables.

Theme 4) Making notes

Objectives
Text level:
- 7 describe and sequence key incidents
- 17 make clear notes: discussing and identifying purposes; identifying key words; exploring ways of writing in shortened forms; making use of simple formats to capture key points

Sentence level:
- 9 experiment with deleting words in sentences

Resources
Enlarged text versions of notes in various formats, serving various purposes. An enlarged non-fiction extract including a substantial amount of text; photocopies of this and similar texts for children to mark up. A message in telegram style. Copymasters 27 & 28. Homework 14.

Assessment
At the end of this theme is the pupil able to:
- identify and discuss the purpose of note-making in general and in specific cases;
- make clear notes using a range of different techniques and formats;
- capture key ideas in a few words only;
- distinguish between essential and inessential words in a sentence?

Lesson 1

Whole class

Display enlarged text versions of notes, *e.g. a 'to do' list, a story plan, key facts about an animal.* Prompt children to identify and discuss the purpose and nature of these texts, stressing the idea that they record key points in a few words, acting as 'reminders'. Introduce the term 'notes', and explain that in these lessons they will be learning how to make notes in different ways and for different purposes.

Choose a familiar story, and ask children to work in pairs to list the first three key incidents in note form. Choose pairs to share their lists. Compare and discuss the incidents chosen; distinguish between key incidents and incidents of lesser importance.

Write up one of the lists; work together to record the ideas in fewer words. Present these in different ways, *e.g. as numbered or bulleted points.*

Give pairs of children time-out to rewrite their list, making sure they have only key incidents and trying to express them in fewer words.

Group and independent work
Children choose a familiar story, and record key incidents from it in note form. Towards the end of the session; ask them to read their lists, and see if they can delete any incidents or words.

Differentiation
Low Attainers – continue noting key incidents in the story used in whole-class work.
High Attainers – set a maximum number of words for noting each incident, for example five.

Plenary
Choose children to begin retelling their story from the notes they have made.
Write up selected notes and continue working on making them shorter.

Lesson 2

Whole class

Read an enlarged copy of a non-fiction extract with the children. Ask: *What are the main things you have found out?* Share ideas; find the points in the text where this information is provided.

Explain that identifying key facts is an important skill in reading non-fiction. Work through the first part of the text, identifying key facts and highlighting relevant words and phrases. Explain that instead of marking books (which they shouldn't do!) they can note down key words. Return to the highlighted text, and demonstrate this strategy.

Give pairs of children a photocopy of this text (and of following paragraphs if appropriate) and ask them to read on, identifying main facts, underlining key words, and recording them in as few words as possible.

Choose a pair and ask: *What are the first words you have highlighted?* Prompt others to compare this with their own notes. Repeat this process, focusing on identification of the main facts and highlighting and recording only key words.

Group and independent work
Give children photocopies of other non-fiction extracts, differentiated for reading level. Ask them to go through the text identifying main facts and underlining key words. Then make a brief note of each point.

Differentiation
Low Attainers – underline only key words.
High Attainers – give children a specific focus for note-making.

Plenary
Display an enlarged text copy of one of the extracts. Choose a specific focus of interest; go through the text identifying relevant facts/words. Repeat for another focus.

Lesson 3

Whole class

Write up a relatively long sentence which provides a good deal of information. Ask the children to identify the main idea. Ask: *which words could we get rid of and still keep this idea?* Experiment with crossing out words; re-read the 'new' sentences, and check that they still make sense and that the main idea is retained.
Write up another sentence of this kind, and ask children to write a shortened version which keeps the main idea. Share and compare attempts at this, and write one together.
Look at long and short versions of the two sentences; identify and discuss the kinds of words that can be deleted (generally adjectives, adverbs, 'the', 'a'), distinguishing between ones which are essential to the meaning and ones which are not.
Explain the idea of telegrams: because each word has to

be paid for, only the absolutely essential ones are used. Read the text of a telegram; write a full version of the sentence(s). Experiment with writing telegram versions, e.g. of a school routine.

Group and independent work

Children choose a passage without dialogue in their current reading book, and write a shortened version of it. Write a telegram version of the beginning of a familiar traditional story.

Differentiation

Low Attainers – provide sentences similar to those in whole class work for children to shorten and rewrite.
High Attainers – Copymaster 27: write telegram message from characters in traditional stories.

Plenary

Set this scenario: words cost 10p each; we have £1.00. Write messages related to situations in traditional stories, or recent school events.

Lesson 4

Whole class

Introduce and explain the term 'flow-chart'; if possible, show an example from a non-fiction book. Choose a familiar process or system with clearly identifiable 'steps', *e.g. writing a new document on the computer; lunch-time routines.* Use shared writing techniques to begin writing and designing a flow chart that records these steps. Explain the use of arrows to show links and points of divergence. Revisit the issue of recording ideas in few words. Ask pairs of children to write the next steps. Share and discuss, and complete the flow-chart.
Prompt children to share what they know about two animals (minibeasts are ideal for this purpose). Explain that this information can be organised and recorded in note form using a chart. Write up a chart with column headings for relevant features – *e.g. wings, legs, food, shell* – and row headings for type of animal. Work together

to fill the chart, entering numbers or words in each cell. Ask questions which prompt children to draw on the information in the chart.

Group and independent work

Copymaster 28: Read the descriptions of three alien creatures; design and complete a chart to record the information systematically. Invent another, and add to the chart. Work with large sheets of paper that can be shared.

Differentiation

Low Attainers – provide a chart with appropriate layout and headings.
High Attainers – after completing the chart, invent a fifth alien creature and record information about it.

Plenary

Share and compare ways in which children have designed the charts.
Work together to invent other alien creatures, and record information using one of the formats devised.

Lesson 5

Whole class

Choose two things or animals that can be readily compared; prompt children to identify and discuss the similarities and differences. Explain that this information can be organised and recorded on a chart. Draw up and talk through a chart that has columns for the two things being compared and rows for the features/aspects, *e.g. for animals: habitat, home, food, young.* Work together to fill in the chart. Identify and discuss ways in which the information can now be more easily interrogated and used; ask questions to prompt this.
Choose an issue for debate, *e.g. school uniforms.* Briefly share arguments for and against. Draw up a simple two-column chart, and record parallel 'for' and 'against' arguments across the columns. Remind children about recording key points in a few words. Ask pairs of children to divide a piece of paper into two columns and record

other 'for' and 'against' arguments. Share and discuss; add to the class chart, expressing points as briefly as possible.

Group and independent work

Children use one of these formats to record information or arguments about subjects of their own choice. Provide a list of suitable subjects for comparison or debate. (Later, these could be used during an oral debate or as the basis for a piece of writing.)

Differentiation

Low Attainers – provide the beginning of a comparison chart with some headings.
High Attainers – complete a 'for' and 'against' chart with arguments matched across the columns.

Plenary

Swap charts between partners; give the children a couple of minutes of reading; then choose children to present a chart; ask the children to explain what information it provides and how.

Theme 5) Myths and legends

Objectives

Text level:
- 1 investigate the styles and voices of traditional story language
- 2 identify story themes
- 7 describe and sequence key incidents in a variety of ways
- 9 write a story plan for a myth

Sentence level:
- 2 recognise the function of adjectives in sentences
- 3 use the term 'adjective'
- 9 experiment with deleting words

Word level:
- 7 practise new spellings
- 8 understand how words change when *y* is added
- 17 collect new words from reading
- 18 infer the meaning of unknown words from context

Resources
A collection of traditional and modern myths about how animals came to be as they are. Suitable modern myths are Rudyard Kipling's *Just So Stories* and Ted Hughes's *How the Whale Became*. Enlarged text extracts from some of these stories. A recording of the story used in Lesson 1. A story-ladder planning format. Copymasters 29 & 30. Homework 15.

Assessment
At the end of this theme is the pupil able to:
- discuss traditional stories of this type, identifying recurring and significant features;
- identify the key incidents in a story and record them in a variety of ways;
- generate adjectives to describe animals, showing understanding of their use in sentences;
- turn nouns into adjectives by adding the suffix *y*, following the related spelling rules;
- use context to work out the meaning of new words encountered in reading;
- express ideas concisely in note form, deleting unnecessary words?

Lesson 1

Whole class

In this theme the children will be reading myths about how animals came to be as they are, and writing their own. Read to the children a short traditional 'how the animal became' story. Encourage them to respond to the story freely. Prompt the children to consider why people made up and told stories of this kind.

Display the story-ladder 'blank', and explain how this can be used to record the main incidents in a story. Record the first event in note form on the ladder.

Give pairs of children time-out to note the next two or three main events. Share and agree on these; emphasise the importance of recording ideas concisely, experimenting with deleting words so that only the essential idea remains. Read an enlarged text version of some of the story together; explain and model strategies for working out new words. Identify and highlight adjectives, especially ones used to describe the animal featured in the story.

Group and independent work
Children read the beginning of other stories of this kind; they record the main events on a story ladder. Choose and write down a favourite sentence.

Differentiation
Low Attainers – children listen to the story on audio tape as they follow the text.
High Attainers – in addition, children note adjectives used to describe the animal.

Plenary
Ask children to share their favourite sentences, explaining why they have chosen them; prompt them to relate this both to the plot and to the use of words.

Lesson 2

Whole class

Read all or some of a modern 'how the animal became' story. Discuss any similarities and differences between this and the story read in Lesson 1.

Give children time to read an enlarged text extract from the story independently, and to note adjectives and words new to them. Re-read together. As in Lesson 1, model strategies for inferring the meaning of new words; develop this by listing possibilities. Identify the adjectives. Cover them up; re-read the sentences without them, and discuss the differences. Ask children to identify the first main event in the story. Record as a sentence; ask children which words could be removed. Experiment with this, covering up words and re-reading.

Introduce and model a different technique for recording events, *e.g. a labelled map or simple storyboard*.

Give pairs time-out to record remaining key events in the fewest possible words. Share, considering both the sequence of incidents and the way in which they are expressed.

Group and independent work
Children read the story from Lesson 1, recording main events. Note other favourite sentences, and decide which comes 'top of their list'.

Differentiation
Low Attainers – continue listening to and following the recorded story.
High Attainers – record events using the technique introduced in whole-class work. Continue noting adjectives.

Plenary
Choose children to share their record of events. Write up some and experiment together with deleting words. Continue to share and discuss favourite sentences.

Lesson 3

Whole class

Suggest possibilities for a new 'how the animal became' story, identifying animal and feature(s), *e.g. the cat's whiskers, the elephant's ears*.

Give pairs of children time-out to discuss other ideas, then share them as a class. Choose one to develop together.

Write up the name of the animal, and ask children to record adjectives to describe it. Compile a class list. Encourage children to search their vocabularies for vivid, interesting words. Model strategies for attempting the spelling of new words.

Highlight adjectives which are formed by adding *y* to nouns, *e.g. woolly, shiny*. (Add words to illustrate this if necessary.) Ask children what they notice about these words; explain how they are formed, and the related

spelling rules (drop final e; double final consonant in words ending CVC).

Group and independent work

Children choose an animal for their own story, and write a of list adjectives to describe it. Write up nouns which form the basis of adjectives ending with *y*, illustrating the three spelling patterns; ask children to turn them into adjectives.

Differentiation

Low Attainers – Copymaster 29: turn nouns into adjectives to fill gaps in sentences.

High Attainers – write and design a poster explaining and illustrating the spelling rules.

Plenary

Choose children to read their list of adjectives; ask others to guess what the animal is.

Choose from this list adjectives ending in *y*; ask children to identify the noun from which they are formed.

Lesson 4

Whole class

Explain that in this lesson they will be planning the new story. Remind children of the animal and the feature(s). Write up questions to help them focus on key issues for this story (see Copymaster 30).

Organise the class into small groups and give them time-out to develop a storyline. Ask groups to present their idea. Discuss, and choose one to develop.

Plan the plot together, using one of the formats from the first two lessons to record key events in order. Before writing these down, ask children if they can find a shorter way of expressing the idea, and experiment with deleting words.

Focus on the moment of transformation and plan it in more detail.

Group and independent work

Children plan their own individual 'how the *x* became'

story, drawing on whole-class work and using Copymaster 30 to record their ideas. Towards the end of this phase, ask children to swap plans with a partner and discuss; explain that each has the task of suggesting improvements.

Differentiation

Low Attainers – use the whole-class plan, changing some elements and/or introducing new ones.

High Attainers – choose their own planning format, and, as in whole-class work, plan the transformation in more detail.

Plenary

Ask pairs of children who worked together during the independent phase to present each other's story plans, explaining how they might be improved. Prompt others to join in the discussion.

Lesson 5

Whole class

Choose one of the stories read in Lessons 1 and 2 to serve as the language model for the new story. Read the beginning (in an enlarged text version if possible) and prompt children to discuss language features.

Give children time-out to compose (orally or on paper) the opening sentence for the class story; encourage higher attainers to write in the style of the original. Share and discuss sentences.

Use shared writing techniques to compose the early part of the story, focusing on what the animal was like. Focus children's attention on adjectives; experiment with the effect of different choices.

Move on to the transformation, and write this episode together. Look for opportunities to revisit spelling strategies for new words and adjectives ending in *y*.

Group and independent work

Children begin writing the story which they planned in Lesson 4. When they have drafted the first few sentences, they swap with their partner, and discuss strengths and points for improvement.

This provides an opportunity for more extended writing which children could pursue in other Literacy Hours and/or outside this context.

Differentiation

Low Attainers – tell the story in a limited number of sentences, *e.g. one to describe the situation at the start; two for the transformation; one for situation at the end*.

High Attainers – encourage children to use language structures from the story read at the start of the lesson.

Plenary

Monitor children's writing to choose examples that illustrate teaching points about plot development and use of adjectives. Share and discuss.

Theme 6) Performance poetry

Objectives

Text level:
- 4 choose and prepare poems for performance
- 5 rehearse and improve performance, taking note of punctuation
- 11 write new or extended verses for performance based on models of performance poetry read

Sentence level:
- 6 note where commas occur in reading, and discuss their functions in helping the reader
- 7 use the term 'comma' in relation to reading

Word level:
- 1 revise spelling of words containing long vowel phonemes
- 4 discriminate syllables in reading
- 6 use independent spelling strategies: sounding out and spelling phonemes

Resources
Enlarged text versions of two 'performance poems' both organised in verses, but contrasting in structure, rhythm, rhyme, pace, mood. A range of other poems suitable for performance. Cards with the different spellings for long vowel phonemes and a selection of consonants and consonant clusters and digraphs.
Copymasters 31 & 32. Homework 16.

Assessment
At the end of this theme is the pupil able to:
- read poems with appropriate rhythm, pace and intonation;
- work with others to plan, rehearse and improve a read-aloud poetry performance;
- take account of commas and other punctuation marks when reading aloud;
- discriminate and count syllables in words and in lines of poetry;
- write new lines and verses modelled on structures of poems read;
- spell words with long vowel phonemes accurately?

Lesson 1

Whole class

Read the first poem in a dull, hesitant, unrhythmic manner. Ask children what they notice. Explain that you read it like this on purpose and that in these lessons they will be working together to perform poems effectively. Show the enlarged text of the first poem, and give children a few minutes to read it independently. Ask for volunteers to read one verse aloud. Comment on the strengths of these readings, *e.g. appropriate rhythm, pauses, stresses.* Read and re-read the poem together as a class, discussing how lines and verses should 'go'. Explain how the punctuation provides a guide for reading. Focus in particular on commas, highlighting these on the text. Revise the term 'comma'.
Write up sentences in which commas are used in various simple ways; ask pairs to read them together. Then choose children to read sentences aloud; explain and model how commas guide phrasing.

Group and independent work
Give copies of a performance poem to each group, differentiating these according to attainment in reading. Ask children to read them together, focusing on rhythm etc., and to begin experimenting with ways of sharing out the text between them.
Ask each child to find a sentence with a comma or commas in his or her current reading book, and to practise it.

Differentiation
Low Attainers – Copymaster 31: highlight commas in sentences, and practise reading them.
High Attainers – practise reading a page in their books, paying special attention to punctuation.

Plenary
Choose children to read sentences with commas; write up some, highlight the commas, and model correct phrasing.

Lesson 2

Whole class

Read the first verse of the second, contrasting poem aloud while the children follow the text. Explain and re-read lines to show the appropriate phrasing, rhythm, pace, expression, etc. and how you use punctuation. Organise the class into groups of five or six, and give them time-out to practise reading the poem together. Then ask each group to read out loud; invite other children to comment, starting with positive points. Re-read the poem together, drawing on these group readings to improve the performance.
Display the text of both poems. Divide the class into two groups and assign a poem to each. Give children time-out to formulate ideas individually; prompt them to think about what the poem 'says' and how it is written. Ask each group to present ideas about their poem.

Group and independent work
Give groups five minutes to continue working on the performance of their poem. Next they record it; listen to and evaluate their reading; discuss ways of improving it; and perform it again. (An alternative would be for one child in the group to act as a critical listener, and report to the others.)

Differentiation
Low Attainers – join in to support the reading; prompt children to focus on key issues.
High Attainers – challenge children to produce a polished taped recording of the poem.

Plenary
Choose groups to share their first recorded attempt, and then perform the improved version. Ask others to comment on the differences.

Lesson 3

Whole class

Remind children of previous work on words with long vowel phonemes; generate and write up a few examples for each, organising them in columns.

Display the text of both poems, and ask children to write down any words with long vowel phonemes. Work through the poems together, highlighting these words and writing them in the appropriate column.

Take the column with most words, and identify any different ways of spelling the phoneme. Give pairs time-out to identify other spellings for this phoneme, and to record two words which illustrate each. Share words; compile organised lists for the phoneme in question; add other patterns to complete the picture if necessary. Give each pair a long vowel phoneme card and ask them to write down words in which it occurs. Choose a

group to share their words; check for accuracy; write up.

Group and independent work

Organise groups to work on another long vowel phoneme, compiling an organised list of different spellings as in whole-class work.

Differentiation

Low Attainers – make and record words using two or three phoneme cards plus selected consonants and consonant clusters.

High Attainers – Copymaster 32: explore vowel phonemes by listing rhyming words with same/different spelling patterns.

Plenary

Say words with long vowel phonemes and ask children to suggest rhymes; record these; draw out different spelling patterns.

Lesson 4

Whole class

Read or re-read an enlarged text of a performance poem with strong rhythmic patterns. Repeat some lines, stressing these patterns. Highlight words or parts of words on which the stresses fall.

Explain that rhythm in poetry depends on the pattern of these stresses and the number of syllables in a line. Revise syllables by asking children to write words with 1, 2, 3, 4 syllables: first, any words; then words in the poem. Share words; confirming the syllable count. Focus on lines in the poem where patterns of rhythm are strongest, and count the syllables in these lines. Record this from verse to verse, and identify the pattern that emerges.

Use shared writing strategies to compose new lines with the same number of syllables and the same rhythm. Read aloud to check.

Group and independent work

The children choose a category, and write a list of words with 1, 2, 3, 4 syllables.

They work out and record the pattern of syllables in the poem they performed, *e.g. writing numbers at the end of each line.*

Differentiation

Low Attainers – sort a set of word cards by the number of syllables; then add two more.

High Attainers – find a word with 5 syllables; write new lines with the same number of syllables and the same rhythm.

Plenary

Share, write up, read and check words with 1, 2, 3, 4, 5 syllables.

Ask children who have written new lines to read the original and their own versions.

Lesson 5

Whole class

Choose one of the performance poems read in this unit to use as a model for writing. Re-read it together; identify and discuss the main features of language and structure.

Choose a line or pair of lines with a simple pattern. Experiment with changing individual words to express a different meaning, but retain the language patterns. Move on from this to write complete new versions of the line or lines.

Discuss possibilities for writing a new verse for the poem. Ask: What could the subject be? Share ideas, and choose one.

Generate and record words related to this subject. If the poem rhymes, look for rhyming pairs.

Use shared writing techniques to compose a new verse. At appropriate points, give children time-out to write

lines on their own; then draw on contributions to develop the shared text.

Group and independent work

Children write a new verse for the poem they performed earlier in the unit. This could be organised as individual or collaborative work.

Practise reading the new verse aloud.

Differentiation

Low Attainers – identify a line or lines for children to replace; copy out the new verse that results.

High Attainers – write a complete new verse on a different subject.

Plenary

Choose children or groups to read the whole poem aloud, incorporating their new or adapted verses. Discuss how well the new verse fits in. Discuss the effectiveness of performances

Theme 7) Pluralisation

Objectives

Sentence level:
- 4 extend knowledge and understanding of pluralisation
- 5 use the terms 'singular' and 'plural' 'appropriately'
- 10 understand the differences between verbs in the first, second and third persons
- 11 understand the need for grammatical agreement

Word level:
- 7 practise new spellings
- 9 investigate and identify basic rules for changing the spelling of nouns when s is added
- 11 use the terms 'singular' and 'plural' appropriately

Resources
Enlarged text extracts from familiar kinds of writing in the first person, e.g. diary or letter, the second person, e.g. instructions or advice, and the third person, e.g. a story. An enlarged text including errors in agreement between subject and verb, e.g. They was, She come. Copymasters 33 & 34. Homework 17.

Assessment
At the end of this theme is the pupil able to:
- understand the meaning of the terms 'singular' and 'plural';
- know and use the basic spelling rules for pluralisation of nouns;
- spell common irregular plural nouns accurately;
- write sentences in which the subject and verb are in grammatical agreement, and identify errors in agreement;
- write consistently and accurately in the first, second and third persons?

Lesson 1

Whole class

Demonstrate the idea of 'singular' and 'plural' in concrete terms, e.g. by holding up one and then more than one pen, asking children to say what they see, and recording this: one pen, (two, lots of) pens.
Ask pairs of children to look round the classroom, and to identify three things there is only one of and three things where there is more than one; they then write the words down.
Share and write up the plural words. Use this list (adding to it as necessary) to explain and demonstrate the basic spelling rules for pluralisation of nouns, focusing on words ending in sh, ch, tch and x (add es) and in y preceded by a consonant (change y to i before adding es). Write up a selection of words that illustrate the application of these rules, and ask children to write the plural forms.

Group and independent work
Read a book until the children have found three plural and three singular nouns; write down the words. Write singular and plural forms of three nouns with each of the following endings: s, sh, ch, tch, x, vowel + y, consonant + y. Present this on a task-board or as a worksheet.

Differentiation
Low Attainers – give children lists of words to pluralise.
High Attainers – write and design a poster explaining and illustrating the spelling rules for pluralisation.

Plenary
Pool plural forms of words with each of the endings; confirm correct spelling.
Ask children who have written rules to read them; ask others if they are accurate and helpful.

Lesson 2

Whole class

Write up sentences including a word with an irregular plural form, e.g. children, men, feet, mice, making it clear from the wording that each of these refers to more than one thing. Read the sentences together. Highlight these plural nouns, and ask children what they notice. Draw out the idea that these words refer to plural objects but do not end in s. Ask children to write the singular form. Share and confirm. Generate other pairs of nouns in which the plural form is irregular. Practise these spellings using the 'look, say, cover, write, check' method.
Write up sentences including words such as sheep, rubbish, scissors and trousers, using them in the singular. Ask children to try rewriting the sentences in the plural, e.g. by adding the phrase 'lots of'. Ask them what they notice. Explain that these nouns are the same in the singular and the plural. List other such words, e.g. for clothing: shorts, jeans, trunks, pants.

Group and independent work
Write up a list of nouns with irregular pluralisation, some in the singular and some in the plural. Ask children to complete the pairs, and to use one of the words in a sentence.

Differentiation
Low Attainers – Copymaster 33: fill gaps in the sentences with common irregular plural nouns.
High Attainers – write and illustrate a one-to-ten 'tricky counting book' using nouns with irregular plurals.

Plenary
Carry out a short irregular plurals test, asking children to write down the word that completes sentences in the form: 'One tooth but two ____' . Share and check the spelling of answers.

Lesson 3

Whole class

Write up some common collective nouns related to school life, *e.g. class, group*. Explain that these nouns are singular but relate to collections of people. Give children time-out to think of other such words; share and record.
Write up the names of two or three animals *e.g. cows, bees, sheep* and the corresponding collective nouns – *herd, swarm, flock*. Ask children to match them. Introduce the term 'collective nouns' for words which describe a collection of people or animals.
Write up some less established, more playful collective nouns, *e.g. a giggle of girls, a slither of snakes, a worry of mothers*, and discuss their meaning and appropriateness. List a few other animals and categories of people, *e.g. babies, parents, teenagers*, and ask children to work in pairs to think of collective nouns for them. Share and discuss ideas.

Group and independent work

Write up other collective nouns for animals, *e.g. pack, school, gaggle, litter, pride*, and ask children to find the animals they refer to, using a dictionary if they need help.
Write up a list of more animals and categories of people and ask children to invent collective nouns for them.

Differentiation

Low Attainers – match cards with collective nouns and related animal words; write out the resulting phrases.
High Attainers – invent collective nouns for animals and people of their own choice.

Plenary

Confirm the pairings of animals and collective nouns that you listed.
Ask children to share collective nouns they have found for particular animals or categories of people; choose favourites.

Lesson 4

Whole class

Write up the personal pronouns *I, you, he, she, we, they*. Ask children to write these in two sets: singular and plural. Ask: *What do you notice about 'you'?* Explain that it is both singular and plural.
Now regroup the pronouns into the first person (I, we); second person (you); and third person (he, she, they). Organise the class into three groups, and ask each to write sentences beginning with one of these sets of pronouns; assign 'you' to the Higher Attainers.
Share these sentences, group by group, and write up some. Note examples where there is lack of grammatical agreement between pronoun and verb, and correct. (This will be developed in the next lesson.)
Show the enlarged text extracts in each 'person'. Prompt children to identify the pronouns, and highlight them. Identify the purpose and genre of each piece of writing. Use shared writing techniques to continue each text for a couple of sentences; draw attention to use of pronouns and matching verb forms.

Group and independent work

Write a short text in each of the three genres used in whole-class work. You could support this by setting appropriate subjects.

Differentiation

Low Attainers – provide starter sentences for each genre to establish the style.
High Attainers – highlight pronouns and verbs as the children write, and check that they 'match'.

Plenary

Choose children to share what they have written in each genre; work together to add a few more sentences, drawing attention to use of pronouns and verbs.

Lesson 5

Whole class

Write up a sentence featuring singular nouns, *e.g. The postman was carrying a heavy bag*. Work together to change the sentence into the plural: *The postmen were …* Ask children to identify all the words that change.
Write up other singular sentences, chosen to represent different tenses and pronouns, and ask children to write plural versions. Share and check the plural sentences, again highlighting words that change, focusing in particular on pluralisation of nouns and pronouns and change in the form of main and auxiliary verbs. Emphasise that these need to 'agree'.
Display the text including deliberate errors in agreement. Read it together; pause to identify and correct the first mistake. Then ask children to identify the others independently, sentence by sentence, writing down the correct word. Confirm the correct forms.

Group and independent work

Write up a list of singular nouns chosen to represent different spelling rules for adding s. Ask children to choose three, and to write sentences including them. Then transform them into the plural. Underline all the words that change.

Differentiation

Low Attainers – Copymaster 34: transform 'singular' sentences into the 'plural'.
High Attainers – write a short text about one child, and rewrite so that it features three.

Plenary

Use shared writing techniques to rewrite the beginning of *Goldilocks and the Three Bears*, so that there is only one bear. Focus on correct and consistent use of pronouns and verbs.

Theme 8 Traditional stories

Objectives

Text level:
- 1 investigate the styles and voices of traditional stories
- 2 identify typical story themes
- 3 identify and discuss main and recurring characters
- 9 write a story plan for own traditional tale
- 10 write sequels to traditional stories

Sentence level:
- 2 recognise the function of adjectives within sentences; experiment with deleting and substituting; collect and classify
- 8 recognise other uses of capitalisation

Word level:
- 13 recognise and spell common suffixes

Resources
A variety of traditional stories in picture book editions

and collections; some that are familiar and some that are new. Enlarged text extracts from a selected story, in particular to illustrate typical language features (see Lesson 2). Cards with typical openings, transitions (e.g. *from one time or place to another*) and endings. Copymasters 37 & 38. Homework 19.

Assessment
At the end of this theme is the pupil able to:
- identify and discuss the typical language features of traditional tales;
- identify recurring themes and characters in traditional tales, and compare them across stories;
- draw on reading to write a sequel and plan own traditional tale;
- choose and use adjectives to describe characters, showing understanding of their function;
- read and spell words (adverbs) ending with the suffix *ly*?

Lesson 1

Whole class

In this theme the children will be explaining traditional stories and writing their own version of one.
Read children the beginning of a traditional story which is unfamiliar but includes typical themes, characters, settings and language. Ask: *What kind of story is this? How do we know?* In discussion, draw attention to typical features and ask children to suggest other stories in which they occur. List the characters in this story, and ask children, working in pairs, to list other characters commonly encountered in traditional stories.
Compile a class list. As you do so, explain use of capital letters at the start of proper names (Cinderella), contrasting this with generic characters (step-mothers). Write up adjectives that describe these characters, e.g. *beautiful, cruel, brave, clever, foolish*. Revise or introduce the term 'adjective'. Give children time-out to think of other adjectives to describe characters from traditional stories.

Choose one of the characters, and discuss him/her in more detail, prompting children to comment on his/her role in various stories.

Group and independent work
Children choose and write down the name of a character from traditional tales; write down the title of the story or stories that he/she features in; and list adjectives to describe.

Differentiation
Low Attainers – Copymaster 37: match adjectives to a character; choose one and name stories that he/she features in.
High Attainers – in addition, write a short description of their chosen character.

Plenary
Share characters; write up their names, noting whether they begin with a capital letter; share adjectives to describe them.
Choose a child to read a portrait without revealing the name of the character; ask others to work this out.

Lesson 2

Whole class

Read an enlarged text of the beginning of a traditional story with typical language features. Ask: *How can we tell this is a traditional tale just by the way it is written?* Identify typical words and phrases.
Distribute cards with openings, transitions and endings, explaining these three functions. Ask children to sort themselves into three groups; give higher attainers the 'transition' cards. Ask groups to read out their cards. Write up the question: 'How do traditional tales usually end?' Ask children what they notice about the word 'usually': explain addition of *ly* to the adjective 'usual'. Introduce or revise the term 'suffix'. Write up the common ending 'happily ever after'. Explain the spelling pattern. Write up adjectives that follow these two patterns; give children time-out to add *ly* to these words; confirm correct spellings.

Group and independent work
Distribute traditional tales, ideally to pairs of children; ask them to read the beginning of the story, and to note down how it starts and other language features. Then read and note the ending of the story.
Write up a list of adjectives for the children to change into adverbs.

Differentiation
Low Attainers – Copymaster 38: match sentences from three well-known tales, and give the title.
High Attainers – give children a selection of the cards with openings and endings; ask them to 'scan' a collection of texts looking for stories that use them.

Plenary
Ask children to share any new openings and endings they have found.
Carry out a short adverbs spelling test. Check answers; revise spelling rules.

Lesson 3

Whole class

Choose a familiar story that exemplifies a common theme of traditional tales. e.g. *The Three Little Pigs* (weak over strong); *Anansi* stories (clever over foolish); *Rumpelstiltskin* (passing a test).

Give children time-out to recall and retell the story with a partner. Briefly confirm outline of plot, *e.g. by listing key events*. Ask questions that prompt children to move on from 'what happens' to 'what the story is about', *e.g. What do you think is the main idea behind the story? What did the people who told this story want to say about the world?* Draw on contributions to write up a short statement of the 'theme'; introduce and explain this term.

Write up the titles of two or three other familiar stories, and give children time-out to discuss and record themes of these stories. Share ideas, and agree on the themes; write them up, next to the story titles. Discuss why these are common themes.

Group and independent work

Children choose a traditional tale; recall/re-read it; and write a sentence stating its theme.

Differentiation

Low Attainers – give children cards stating a common theme; ask them to find stories which share it; make a small display of books if possible.
High Attainers – find two stories with the same theme; state it in a way that fits both.

Plenary

Taking themes in turn, ask children to suggest stories that illustrate them, briefly explaining how.

Lesson 4

Whole class

Choose a story read and/or discussed in previous lessons or during story-time. Review characters, setting, plot and theme.

Ask children what they think might happen next. Model this by suggesting continuations of familiar stories from work in previous lessons, *e.g. Goldilocks might come back to apologise to the bears; the giant might climb down the beanstalk and try to get into Jack's house.* Give children, working in pairs, time-out to discuss possibilities for the chosen story. Encourage them to keep within the world of traditional stories.

Share ideas. Agree on one to develop together.

Use shared writing techniques to plan and begin drafting a sequel. Prompt children to make use of the language structures identified in Lesson 2, and to incorporate these in the story, especially at transition points and at the end.

Group and independent work

Children choose a traditional story and write a sequel for it. Display the language structure cards for them to refer to.

Differentiation

Low Attainers – children develop one of the other ideas for continuing the story discussed in whole-class work; they could record on tape rather than write their sequel.
High Attainers – challenge children to use at least three of the language structures in their sequel and to introduce a new character.

Plenary

Choose children to read their sequels, or do this for them. Discuss whether it fits with the original story, using this to revisit teaching points about typical elements. Identify uses of typical language features that make it 'sound like' a traditional tale.

Lesson 5

Whole class

Review the themes identified and discussed in Lesson 3. Agree on one as the basis for writing a new traditional tale. Write up headings for 'setting', 'characters', 'plot'. Give pairs of children time-out to begin developing a story, considering these elements.

Share ideas, listing possibilities under each heading, and agree on a story outline. Plan the sequence of events, recording this as a story ladder or list. Brainstorm and record adjectives to describe the main characters. Display the openings cards. Ask children to choose one and compose a first sentence on their whiteboards. Choose children to read ones starting in different ways. Use shared writing techniques to draft the first episode. Look for opportunities to use other typical language features and adjectives to describe the main characters.

Group and independent work

Children develop their own story, based on the theme discussed, but choosing their own setting, characters and plot. Plan this by listing the main events and adjectives to describe the main characters. Write the first sentence. (This provides a starting point for more extended writing which children could pursue in other Literacy Hours and/or outside this context.)

Differentiation

Low Attainers – base their story on the one planned in whole-class work, varying one or two elements.
High Attainers – identify the key moment in their story and plan it in more detail.

Plenary

Choose children to read their opening sentence and to say briefly what is gong to happen in their story. Prompt others to compare this with stories read in the unit, considering characters, settings and incidents.

Theme 9) Reading instructions

Objectives

Text level:
- 12 identify the different purposes of instructional texts
- 13 discuss the merits and limitations of instructional texts to give an overall evaluation
- 14 recognise how written instructions are organised
- 15 read and follow simple instructions

Sentence level:
- 6 note where commas occur in reading and discuss their functions in helping the reader
- 7 use the term 'comma'

Word level:
- 12 recognise and generate compound words
- 24 explore opposites

Resources

A variety of instructional texts: from different sources, *e.g. non-fiction books, consumer leaflets, manuals*; serving different purposes; using different organisational and presentational features. Enlarged text versions of a selection of these.

Purpose-written instructional texts for Lessons 2 and 5. Word cards to put together to make compound word pronouns, for Lesson 2.

Copymasters 35 & 36. Homework 18.

Assessment

At the end of this theme is the pupil able to:
- understand the general purpose of instructional texts, and a range of specific purposes within this genre;
- read and follow simple instructions;
- identify and discuss organisational and presentational features of instructional texts;
- evaluate the effectiveness of particular instructional texts, commenting on relevant issues;
- understand the use of commas in lists;
- understand and generate pairs of opposite words;
- identify and generate compound words?

Lesson 1

Whole class

Give children oral instructions to get organised for this lesson. Ask them what you have been doing. Use the term 'instructions' and remind them of earlier work. Read together an enlarged instructional text; identify and briefly discuss its purpose.

Read aloud extracts from a range of other instructional texts, drawing on examples from inside and outside school. Prompt children to identify the purpose of each. Ask them to share ideas with a partner about instructions they have used themselves and seen in use at home. Share ideas as a class, and compile a list. Write up some compound words, *e.g. inside, underneath*, if possible choosing ones from the instructional texts read. Ask children what they notice, and draw a vertical line between the two parts. Write up words with which common compound words begin, focusing on pronouns, e.g. *every, no, some*, and ask children to add on other words to make compound words. Compile a class list.

Group and independent work

Find and read other instructional texts; write a label identifying their purpose.

Write up other common elements of compound words, and ask children to make compound words by joining them together or adding another element.

Differentiation

Low Attainers – join cards with common elements to make compound words; record these.

High Attainers – read and identify purposes of instructional texts from non-school contexts.

Plenary

Share purposes for instructions children have found, and add new ones to the list begun in whole-class work. Draw on contributions to make organised lists of compound words beginning/ending with the same element.

Lesson 2

Whole class

Display an enlarged text version of instructions which children can follow during the lesson to produce the same outcome, *e.g. for drawing a simple picture or shape*. Give them time out to read and follow the instructions individually and independently.

Ask them to compare finished products in small groups. Ask children to read the instructions out loud, while you record the developing image on the board. Make deliberate mistakes to highlight the importance of careful reading. Identify any points at which the instructions themselves were not clear. Recap work on compound words, and extend this by writing up words with more substantive meanings, e.g. *playground, waterfall, snowman*. Identify the constituent words, and how their meanings are combined, *e.g. a man made of snow.*

Group and independent work

Write up words which start sets of compound words, *e.g. foot, snow, water, head*. Ask children to write lists of words. Read and follow simple instructions, *e.g. for making a book or pop-up card.*

Differentiation

Low Attainers – Copymaster 35: read and follow simple instructions to draw a clown's face.

High Attainers – Copymaster 36: read and follow more complex instructions to draw a pattern.

Plenary

Pool independent work to compile class lists for compound words beginning with the same element. Share and discuss the process of following instructions; look for opportunities to focus on key points, and introduce the idea of evaluating instructional texts.

Lesson 3

Whole class

Read with the children an enlarged text version of instructions which exemplify common language and organisational features of this genre, *e.g. sentences beginning with verbs, lists (of things needed), numbered or bulleted points, diagrams.*

Give the children, working in pairs, time-out to discuss how the text is written. Share ideas as a class, focusing attention on significant features (see above). In each case, prompt children to explain the reasons why the text is written in this way, relating these to the purpose of the instructions and ways of helping the reader. Select, from this or other texts read, words which have clear opposites, *e.g. long, inside, below, straight, full, right,* and write them up. Choose one, and write down the opposite; explain the relationship between the two words, and ask children to provide opposites for the others you have written. Then ask pairs to record other pairs of opposites. Share as a class, and compile a list; identify and discuss any which are not true opposites.

Group and independent work

Look at and read instructions from the collection; identify and record organisational devices used. Set a context, *e.g. weather or shapes,* and ask children to record pairs of opposite words to do with it.

Differentiation

Low Attainers – give children one of a pair of opposite words to complete.
High Attainers – use some pairs of opposites in the same sentence.

Plenary

Pool pairs of opposite words; as before, identify any that are not true opposites.
Choose children to describe devices used in the instructions they looked at; develop discussion of how they help the reader.

Lesson 4

Whole class

Display enlarged text instructions in which diagrams feature.
Read together. Prompt children to identify and discuss the language and organisation, comparing this with the instructions read in Lesson 3.
Focus on the diagrams. Discuss what information they provide and how they relate to the text. Identify accompanying text, *e.g. labels or captions, and the purposes they serve.* Identify any graphical conventions, *e.g. arrows, dotted lines indicating where to fold, scissors indicating 'cut here'.* Extend the range of these by showing other instructions. Ask children to imagine that no diagrams were used: How could they provide the information in words? Give them time-out to try writing this down. Compare results.
Focus on lists of 'what you need' in instructions. Discuss how they are presented. If as a 'running' list with items separated by commas, identify these and recap their function. If in a column, rework this as a running list, adding commas.

Group and independent work

Ask children to write lists of equipment and materials needed to make or do familiar things, *e.g. go swimming, make a cup of tea or a cheese sandwich,* first as a column list, then as a running list using commas.

Differentiation

Low Attainers – make a picture list first.
High Attainers – in addition, find examples in the collection of instructions of these two ways of presenting lists.

Plenary

Use shared writing techniques to write a running list for one of the examples (or a new one); focus on use of commas between items.

Lesson 5

Whole class

Prepare for this lesson by writing a short instructional text in straight prose in which there are deliberate errors in sequencing, completeness and clarity. Choose a subject which they can 'mime' in class, *e.g. cooking baked beans or scrambled eggs on toast.*
Read the text together; pause at each step for children to mime the actions. Prompt them to read carefully, and to do just what the instructions say and nothing else. Identify the problems as they are encountered; relate them to errors of the three kinds noted above. Emphasise these as criteria for effective instructions.
Re-read the instructions step by step; identify ways of changing them so that they are clear, complete and in the right order. Remind children of the organisational devices they investigated in Lessons 3 and 4, and discuss how these could be used to make the instructions more easy to follow.

Group and independent work

Give children instructions which they can use to make something, *e.g. simple paper engineering or book-making.* Ask them to read and follow these, and then to comment, first orally and then in writing, on the effectiveness of the instructions.

Differentiation

Low Attainers – give the instructions a star-rating, and write one or two brief comments.
High Attainers – write a longer evaluation, and suggest ideas for improvement.

Plenary

Lead a whole-class discussion of the quality of the instructions read and followed in independent work, asking questions which focus their attention on key issues. Draw up a check-list of criteria for good instructions.

Theme 10 Writing instructions

Objectives

Text level:
- 16 write instructions

Sentence level:
- 4 extend knowledge and understanding of pluralisation
- 5 use the terms 'singular' and 'plural'
- 6 note where commas occur

Word level:
- 5 identify misspelt words
- 6 use independent spelling strategies
- 9 identify and use basic rules for changing the spelling of nouns when s is added
- 11 use the terms 'singular' and 'plural'

Resources
Enlarged text versions of instructional with characteristic language and organisational features; school and/or class rules. An instructional text in straight prose in which there are errors in the spelling of plural nouns, the use of commas in lists, and the spelling of new or subject-specific vocabulary. You could use the 'deliberate mistakes' text from Theme 9 as the basis for this.
NOTE: Work on this unit should follow that in Theme 9. Copymasters 39 & 40. Homework 20.

Assessment
At the end of this theme is the pupil able to:
- write simple instructions for a range of purposes, using characteristic language and organisational features;
- identify misspelt words in own writing;
- use a range of independent spelling strategies to correct misspellings and to attempt new words;
- understand the use of commas in lists;
- understand the terms 'singular' and 'plural', and basic spelling rules for pluralisation?

Lesson 1
Whole class

Recap work on instructions and explain that in this lesson the class will be writing their own instructional for different kinds of activities.
Show an enlarged text version of school or class rules; explain that these are a special kind of instructions. Prompt children to discuss how they are written and presented, *e.g. repeating patterns in wording/numbering, use of bullet points*, and draw on their knowledge of instructional texts to identify ways they could be improved. Use shared writing techniques to experiment with rewriting and re-presenting the rules.
Ask: *would it help to have any other school or class rules?* Give children, working in pairs, time-out to discuss this, and to decide on and write a new rule. Ask them to record words they want to use but are unsure how to spell.
Share new rules; develop and write up some, using the existing, modified rules as a model.

Pool new words; model and demonstrate strategies for the children to attempt and check their spelling.

Group and independent work
Working on large sheets of paper, ask children to write rules for a particular aspect of school life, *e.g. play-times, dinner-times, assemblies,* modelled on examples from whole-class work. This works well as a group activity in which children first discuss and decide on the rules and then write one each.

Differentiation
Low Attainers – write rules beginning with the word 'Do' or 'Don't'.
High Attainers – write rules for a common outside-school activity, *e.g. going swimming.*

Plenary
Share sets of rules; discuss their clarity and the way they are presented.
Identify and work on the spelling of less familiar words.

Lesson 2
Whole class

Name a place in the school or school grounds. Ask children to discuss with a partner how to get there from the classroom; then choose pairs to explain this; prompt others to listen carefully and note any mistakes or confusions. Record these directions on the board.
Name another place in the school and ask pairs to write directions. As in Lesson 1, ask children to note words they are not sure how to spell.
Swap directions between pairs, and try them out in practice: ask children to do what the directions say and nothing else. (If this is not practicable, ask children to imagine following the route described).
Report back, discussing the accuracy of the directions.
Explain and model the convention of beginning sentences in instructions with verbs, *e.g. walk, turn, go up.*

Identify and work on the spelling of problematic words. Compile a list of words commonly used in directions, *e.g. left, right, across, turn, walk.*

Group and independent work
Ask children to write directions for getting from their house to school, or to some other familiar place in the local neighbourhood, *e.g. park, shops, fish and chip shop.* Display the word-list for children to refer to.

Differentiation
Low Attainers – give children opportunities to talk through the directions in pairs before writing.
High Attainers – Copymaster 39: plot routes on a map, and write directions for following them.

Plenary
Share and discuss examples of writing which highlight points of clarity and presentation.
Practise spelling of words commonly used in this context.

Lesson 3
Whole class

Read together an enlarged text version of a recipe. Identify and discuss the language and organisational devices used, focusing on how they help the reader. Choose something which the children have cooked in school or are likely to know how to make. Give pairs a short time-out to discuss this.

Then use shared writing techniques to begin drafting the recipe. Start by writing a running text list of the equipment needed; explain and model use of commas to separate items. Ask pairs to write a similar list for the ingredients. Draw on contributions to write a list together; focus on the placing of commas when items have more than one word, e.g. small tomato, butter, two slices of bread.

Write the first few steps in the recipe, again emphasising clarity, sequencing and completeness, and the general convention of beginning sentences with verbs. Decide together how to present these steps.

Group and independent work

Write up another list of ingredients, without commas, for children to copy and punctuate.

Ask children to write the recipe for something that they know how to make or cook. Encourage them to use organisational devices.

Differentiation

Low Attainers – Copymaster 40: write a text version of a recipe presented in pictures.

High Attainers – use the convention of beginning sentences with verbs.

Plenary

Check punctuation of the list of ingredients.

Choose children to share their recipe; discuss how they have organised and presented it and why.

Practise the spelling of words (especially verbs) commonly used in this context.

Lesson 4
Whole class

Read instructions for making something together. Compare language and organisational devices with those used in the recipe from Lesson 3.

Choose something which the children have recently made, e.g. in Art, or Design and Technology. Talk through the processes involved.

Use shared writing techniques to write a list of materials and tools, setting it out in a column.

Distinguish between items which are 'singular' and 'plural'; introduce and explain these terms.

Using words in the list as the starting point, explain and model the rules for adding s to make singular nouns plural: usually, just add s; add es to words ending in s, x, ch, tch; change y to i before adding es to words ending consonant y.

Write up three words which follow each of these patterns, and ask children to write the plural forms. Share and check.

Work together to draft the first couple of steps in the process, highlighting language and presentational issues.

Group and independent work

Write up lists of other singular nouns which follow the three different rules for adding s; ask children to make these nouns plural.

Ask children to write instructions for something that they know how to make.

Differentiation

Low Attainers – continue and complete the instructions begun in whole-class work.

High Attainers – in addition, write rules for pluralisation, drawing on work from Lesson 1.

Plenary

Check pluralisation of words in the list. Ask children to present their spelling rules; prompt others to discuss their clarity. Agree on a version to display in the classroom.

Lesson 5
Whole class

Display the instructional text with deliberate mistakes, explaining that it needs improvement.

Begin by focusing on editing. Give pairs of children time-out to identify errors in the spelling of plural nouns, the use of commas in lists, and the spelling of new or subject-specific vocabulary. Work through the text line by line, identifying these errors and correcting them. Look for opportunities to reinforce and extend children's knowledge and to set brief time-out tasks to practise what they have learned.

Next, identify points where the instructions are unclear or wrongly sequenced; revise by rewriting and/or marking up the text to show what needs to be changed and how. Finally, focus on organisation and presentation. Prompt children to suggest ways of improving this. Experiment with rewriting sections, using shared writing techniques.

Group and independent work

Ask children to choose one of the instructional texts they wrote in Lessons 1 to 4, and to edit and revise all or some of it.

Differentiation

Low Attainers – set a small number of targets for editing and revision. Alternatively 'mark' the text before the lesson, preferably with the children, indicating points for improvement.

High Attainers – encourage children to focus on ways of improving the clarity of their instructions.

Plenary

Choose children to share their revised texts, explaining what they changed and why.

Monitor independent work to identify common issues in editing and revising the texts; explain and model the relevant processes and knowledge.

Theme 1 Alphabetical texts and indexes

Objectives

Text level:
- 17 scan indexes etc. to locate information
- 18 locate books by classification in class or school libraries
- 21 use IT to bring to a published form
- 24 make alphabetically ordered texts

Sentence level:
- 5 understand how sentences can be joined in more complex ways

Word level:
- 6 use independent spelling strategies: sounding out and spelling using phonemes; by analogy
- 12 collect new words

Resources

A variety of alphabetically organised texts, including general and subject-specific encyclopedias; directories; non-fiction books with more sophisticated indexes, *e.g. sub-sections within main entries.* Enlarged text versions of relevant pages from these.
Copymasters 41 & 42. Homework 21.

Assessment

At the end of this theme is the pupil able to:
- use understanding of classification of books in class and school libraries to find particular titles;
- scan quickly and accurately to find information in alphabetically organised texts;
- plan and write a simple alphabetically organised text;
- use IT to bring a text to published form, considering layout and print styles;
- begin to write non-fiction texts in an impersonal style;
- use a range of strategies to attempt and check the spelling of new words?

Lesson 1

Whole class

If possible, hold this lesson in the school library or resource centre. In this theme the children will be using books and lists that are organised alphabetically.
Write up the title of a fiction book, and ask children how they would find it in the library. Explain that fiction is organised in alphabetical order by the surname of the author, and talk through the process of finding this book on the shelves.
With the children's help, compile a list of the names of ten authors of fiction. Choose one, and ask: *Where would you look for books by this author? Near the beginning of the fiction section? . . . around the middle? . . . towards the end?*
Ask the children to write the authors' names in alphabetical order. Check.
Hold up a non-fiction book, and ask where this goes in the collection. Explain that non-fiction books are organised not alphabetically by author but by subject.

Explain how this system works in your library, referring to any catalogue or listing of subjects. Talk through the process of finding other titles.

Group and independent work

Give children titles of one fiction and one non-fiction book to find in the collection. Write up other titles and ask children to write down where they would look for them.

Differentiation

Low Attainers – give children ten fiction and ten non-fiction books to arrange as they would be in the collection.
High Attainers – Copymaster 41: write notes saying where new books should be placed in the collection.

Plenary

Choose children to explain how they located particular titles, or decided where they should be placed in the collection.
Explain and show where other books, *e.g. poetry, dictionaries,* are to be found.

Lesson 2

Whole class

Introduce a non-fiction book, and show an enlarged text copy of the index. Revise the purpose and organisation of indexes. Explain new features, *e.g. letter headings, sub-sections within main entries.*
Choose a letter section with a large number of entries, and revise ordering of words by second and subsequent letters, *e.g. caterpillar before crocodile.*
Pose a question relevant to the book, and ask children what word they would look for in the index. Explain how to identify a key word to look up. Talk through the process of scanning the index for that word. Focus on how to use letter headings and knowledge of relative positions of letters in the alphabet to avoid scanning the whole index.
Pose another question, and ask pairs of children to write the number of the page where they think the answer will be found. Share, check and model the process again.

Group and independent work

The children imagine they are writing a non-fiction book about a subject they are interested in, and a compile a mini-index.
Give each group a non-fiction book and two relevant questions; ask them to use the index to find the page number where the answer is likely to be, and to record this.

Differentiation

Low Attainers – Copymaster 42: sort names of musical instruments into alphabetical order for an index.
High Attainers – work with more complex questions and indexes with sub-sections within main entries.

Plenary

Choose children to explain how they found the right page. Look for opportunities to explain other issues related to the use of indexes, *eg. what to do if the key word they are looking for is not listed.*

Lesson 3

Whole class

Introduce and show an enlarged text version of a page from an alphabetically organised general encyclopedia. Discuss the purpose of reference books like this, and how information in them is organised.

Read some entries together. Highlight features of layout and print style and how these are designed to help the user. Ask children to comment on the text; draw out the idea that encyclopedias present facts (not opinions) and are impersonal (note absence of pronoun 'I').

Choose a topic, and model the process of finding the entry. Repeat, asking children to tell you what to do. Explain how to use guide words (usually at the tops of pages) and knowledge of relative positions of letters in the alphabet to speed up the search.

Repeat this teaching sequence with an alphabetically organised subject-specific encyclopedia.

Group and independent work

As in the previous lesson, give each group an encyclopedia, and questions. Ask them to find and 'book-mark' pages with the relevant entries, and to write down the answers.

Groups write a question of their own, and swap encyclopedias with another group.

Differentiation

Low Attainers – work with simple questions and texts.
High Attainers – in addition, write a short description of presentational features in the encyclopedia.

Whole class

Ask groups to compare the two encyclopedias they have worked with, focusing on organisation and presentational features.

Lesson 4

Whole class

Explain that in the next two lessons the class will be writing their own mini-encyclopedia. Together, choose an appropriate subject from recent work in another area of the curriculum.

Ask pairs of children to list five key words in this subject. Share, and write up to compile a class-list. Ask: *Are all of these 'key words'?* Identify ones which do not qualify, *e.g. because they are part of or 'come under' other more important words/ideas.* Highlight and/or group words to indicate this.

Ask children to write an alphabetical list of about ten words.

Examine the spelling of the chosen key words, *e.g. listing words with the same phonemes, same spelling patterns, derived words (e.g. wormery from worm).*

Ask children to spell some of these. Check and practise spelling of new or tricky words.

Group and independent work

Ask each group to choose a subject; list ten key words to do with it; check their spelling; and sort the words into alphabetical order.

Choose one of these words, and write down words related to it in ways identified in whole-class work.

Differentiation

Low Attainers – give children a prompt sheet to focus recording of related words.
High Attainers – challenge children to find ten words related to their chosen word in some way.

Plenary

Choose children to present the words they have analysed, *e.g. using the board to write similar words.*

Lesson 5

Whole class

Choose a key word listed in whole-class work in Lesson 4. Give children time-out to think what they would say about it. Share ideas, and write up the main points. Ask children to write the first sentence for an encyclopedia entry.

Use shared writing techniques to draft the entry, if possible using a computer. Focus attention on the use of an impersonal style; on ways of linking sentences; and on checking the spelling of any specialist words. Display again the enlarged text extract from an encyclopedia, and remind children of features of layout and print style. Discuss how they could use features of this kind to make their entry clearer. Experiment with possibilities, and discuss their effects. Decide on a style. (If you cannot use a computer, mark up the handwritten text, indicating print styles and sizes.)

Group and independent work

Group members draft encyclopedia entries for two key words each; share their work; decide on print styles; and bring to a published form and standard. Organise this so that as many children as possible can use computers.

Differentiation

Low Attainers – write just one or two sentences for each key word.
High Attainers – encourage children to write in the style of the encyclopedias they have been reading.

Plenary

Read and discuss work in progress; look for opportunities to extend understanding of the language and presentational styles.

Theme 2) Book reviews

Objectives

Text level:
- 2 refer to significant aspects of the text
- 8 compare and contrast works by the same author
- 9 be aware of authors; discuss preferences and reasons for them
- 14 write book reviews
- 19 summarise orally the content of a text
- 20 write letters (to authors about books)
- 25 revise and extend work on note-making from previous term
- 26 summarise in writing the content of a passage

Sentence level:
- 5 understand how sentences can be joined in more complex ways
- 7 become aware of the use of commas in marking grammatical boundaries within sentences
- revise from previous terms: writing in complete sentences and sentence demarcation

Resources
Enlarged text copy of a book review which covers different aspects of fiction; mixes factual information and opinion; includes sentences with more complex grammatical structures marked by commas. Copies of book reviews, written by yourself, children in previous years, or simple examples taken from magazines. A familiar short novel or story; enlarged text extracts illustrating elements of fiction, *e.g. characterisation, description of setting, plot development.*
Copymasters 43 & 44. Homework 22.

Assessment
At the end of this theme is the pupil able to:
- summarise a story clearly and accurately, orally and in writing;
- express, explain and justify opinions about authors and stories, referring to the text to support and illustrate their ideas;
- plan and write a book review, providing both factual information and expressing opinions;
- link sentences using a wider range of connectives;
- understand how commas show the grammatical structure of sentences, and help the reader 'make sense'?

Lesson 1

Whole class

Display an enlarged text copy of a book review, and ask children to read it out loud, a sentence at a time. After each sentence, re-read together, explaining how to phrase the text so that the meaning is clear.
Highlight commas used to mark grammatical boundaries in a sentence; read, ignoring and then taking account of these commas; explain how they help the reader.
Prompt children to find different elements of the text: examples of factual information and of the reviewer's personal opinion; comments on different aspects of the book, *e.g. characters, plot, style.*
Ask pairs of children to identify the main points made in the review, and to record them in note form. Share and discuss; agree on and write up (say) five key points. Look for ways of noting the point in fewer words.

Group and independent work
Children read copies of other book reviews, and use Copymaster 43 to analyse and comment on them.

Differentiation
Low Attainers – use Copymaster 43 to analyse the review read in whole-class work.
High Attainers – Copymaster 43: in addition, write a short comment on the usefulness of the review.

Plenary
Ask children to share different elements of the reviews they have read drawing on information recorded on their copymasters, *e.g. comments about characters, other books, opinions.*
Discuss what makes a good and useful book review.

Lesson 2

Whole class

Introduce the familiar short novel or story that the children will be reviewing together. Encourage children to share ideas and opinions about it freely. Ask them to imagine that they have just a few seconds to tell someone about the book. What would they say? How would they summarise it? Give a brief time-out for them to think about this, then share and discuss ideas. Distinguish between summarising (capturing the main point) and retelling.
Ask pairs of children to work together to summarise the story in just one sentence; and when they have agreed on one, to write it down.
Share these summaries. Write up some. Check that each does form just one complete sentence, and rewrite as appropriate. Look for opportunities to use commas to show the structure of more complex sentences, explaining how these help the reader. Contribute sentences of this kind yourself, if necessary.

Group and independent work
Ask the children to choose a short novel or story that they know and like and to write a summary of it. Next, ask them to rewrite it to make it as short as they can.

Differentiation
Low Attainers – summarise the story orally for a partner before writing.
High Attainers – challenge the children to summarise their chosen story in just one sentence.

Plenary
Choose children to read their summaries, or do this for them. Write them up; count the sentences; try to rework as one sentence; note points where commas are needed to show the structure of the sentence.

Lesson 3

Whole class

Display an enlarged text extract from the book being reviewed in which characterisation and use of dialogue are highlighted. Ask children to read it out loud, a sentence at a time. As in Lesson 1, re-read together, explaining how to phrase the text so that the meaning is clear. Identify commas used to mark grammatical boundaries in a sentence.

Ask: *What's the author concentrating on in this extract?* Confirm that character and dialogue are of prime importance. Write up questions to focus children's attention on this aspect of fiction, and give pairs time-out to discuss the extract. Share and discuss ideas. Prompt children to focus on what they notice and like/do not like about the characters and how the author describes their feelings, behaviour and relationships. Ask them to refer to the text to support

and illustrate their ideas: *Where can you show us that in the text? Which words make you think that?* Repeat this teaching sequence for other elements of fiction, *e.g. setting, plot development and style.*

Group and independent work

Ask children to re-read parts of the book they have chosen to review, and to make notes under headings for character, setting, plot and style.

Differentiation

Low Attainers – for each aspect, note one thing they notice and one thing they like.
High Attainers – for each aspect, note one text reference or quotation that illustrates their points.

Plenary

Taking each aspect of fiction in turn, choose children to comment on their chosen book, sharing both information and opinions.

Lesson 4

Whole class

Explain that in this lesson they are going to plan and begin writing a review of the book they have been studying in whole-class sessions.

Give individuals or pairs time-out to identify (say) four main points they would make about the book; some could record these. Share and record ideas.

Prompt children to think about ways in which ideas could be organised in a book review, *e.g. strengths/weaknesses; according to the aspects of fiction highlighted in Lesson 3.*

Use shared writing techniques to plan a review. Start by writing headings for each section and for an introduction and conclusion. Then choose one of the main sections, and draw on ideas recorded earlier in the lesson to note down relevant key ideas.

Ask children to compose a sentence for this section.

Share, and develop together to draft the section. Focus on words for linking sentences and places where commas can be used to help the reader.

Group and independent work

Use Copymaster 44 to plan a review organised in terms of aspects of fiction, and begin writing it. This provides an opportunity for more extended writing which children could continue in other contexts.

Differentiation

Low Attainers – write just one sentence for each part of their plan.
High Attainers – draw on notes made in Lesson 3 to illustrate their ideas and support their opinions.

Plenary

Monitor work to choose drafts that you can use to highlight content and organisation of reviews and linking sentences.

Lesson 5

Whole class

Explain that readers sometimes write letters to authors. Give individuals or pairs time-out to think about what they would like to say to the author of the book they have been studying in whole-class sessions. Share ideas, and choose some to record. Identify possibilities, *e.g. thanking the author; saying what you like about the book; relating it to your own life; referring to other books he/she has written; asking questions.*

Explain or revise conventions for letters to an unknown audience, and write school address, date, and appropriate opening.

Use shared writing techniques to compose the letter, drawing on ideas shared earlier in the lesson. As in Lesson 4, discuss how to link sentences, and demonstrate and explain the use of a range of connecting words that can be used instead of 'and' and 'then'. Note points where

commas can be used to help the reader make sense of a sentence.

Group and independent work

Children write a letter to the author of the book they have been reviewing. Write up the school address and a prompt list of 'things to say' (see above) for the children to refer to.

Differentiation

Low Attainers – write about one thing they like and ask one question.
High Attainers – encourage children to develop points about a particular idea.

Plenary

Choose children to read their letters, or extracts from them. Check and discuss whether the style is appropriate.

Plan how to produce revised and edited drafts to post to the author.

Theme 3) Characters

Objectives

Text level:
- 2 refer to significant aspects of the text
- 5 discuss a character's feelings, behaviour and relationships, referring to the text
- 11 write openings to stories linked to reading
- 12 write a first person account

Sentence level:
- 2 identify pronouns and understand their function
- 4 use speech marks and other dialogue punctuation

Word level:
- 11 use the apostrophe to spell shortened forms
- 13 collect synonyms which will be useful in writing dialogue

Resources
A 'core' book in which character and character development are prominent elements. Enlarged text extracts from this book in which feelings and relationships are depicted, including one which depends largely on dialogue.

A collection of other stories in which character is an important element.
Copymasters 45 & 46. Homework 23.

Assessment
At the end of this theme is the pupil able to:
- discuss and comment on the feelings, behaviour and relationships of characters;
- identify a range of ways in which character is depicted, referring to the detail of the text;
- identify and understand the function of pronouns;
- use speech marks and other dialogue punctuation accurately;
- spell shortened forms, placing the apostrophe correctly;
- use a range of words (other than 'said') to set up dialogue;
- draw on reading to plan and write the opening of a story in which character and dialogue are important elements?

Lesson 1
Whole class

Read the first enlarged text extract to the children. Ask: *Who's in the story?* Write up a list, and identify the main character. Ask pairs to re-read the extract, and write up key questions about the main character: *How does she/he feel in this episode? ... behave? ... get on with other characters?* Share responses to these questions. Prompt children to think about how they know about the characters (direct description, dialogue and action).
Identify the character first named in the extract, and track him/her through, highlighting pronouns and other words that refer to that character. Introduce or revise the term 'pronoun'. Repeat for other characters in the episode. List all the pronouns found. Write up a sentence including a name, *e.g. Mrs X is our school keeper.* Then together write a following sentence using an appropriate pronoun, *e.g. She/Her ...* Repeat, asking children to write the next sentences.

Group and independent work
Read another episode where character is important; children list the characters featured and for each write a sentence about how they feel and behave.
Children refer to the whole-class extract and write an account of what the main character does and feels; highlight pronouns.

Differentiation
Low Attainers – focus both activities above on the main character only.
High Attainers – in addition, write a brief description of the main character.

Plenary
Choose children to read their accounts of the main character; ask others to put their hands up when they hear a pronoun; confirm and list.

Lesson 2
Whole class

Read an enlarged text extract from later in the 'core' book. Identify characters involved and develop the discussion of their feelings, behaviour and relationships. Prompt children to identify words and phrases that provide information about this, and compile a list. Highlight the adjectives, and revise their function from Spring Term. Ask children to write other adjectives that could be used to describe the characters. Share and discuss. Ask children to imagine that the main character kept a diary. Explain that this would be in the first person. Give children time-out to draft a sentence from the diary . Share contributions, then use shared writing techniques to develop it. Draw attention to the appropriate pronouns.

Group and independent work
Write a list of adjectives to describe the main character in the episode they read independently in Lesson 1. Write an entry from the diary of another character in the shared text, or from the story read independently.

Differentiation
Low Attainers – continue the main character's diary entry begun in the whole-class phase.
High Attainers – write two diary entries giving contrasting views of the same incident.

Plenary
Share and list adjectives for describing feelings and behaviour. Discuss meanings of less familiar words, and use in sentences.
Choose children to read diary entries; compare content and check consistent use of pronouns.

Lesson 3

Whole class

Read together an extract from the 'core' book which includes a good deal of dialogue. Ask: *Who speaks here?* and identify the characters.

Organise the class into groups of the appropriate number (characters plus narrator), and ask them to re-read the text as a play. Choose a group to present their reading.

Work through the text together, highlighting the dialogue in a different colour for each speaker. Explain the use of speech marks and of other dialogue punctuation to separate words actually spoken from the surrounding narrative. Explain also the layout of the dialogue: new paragraph for each new speaker.

Choose two children to take on the roles of two characters from the story, and to improvise a conversation, *e.g. continuing this episode.* Choose a short, interesting exchange, and used shared writing techniques to record it, demonstrating use of punctuation and layout.

Group and independent work

Organise children in pairs; ask them to choose two other characters (from the shared text or from the story they have read independently) and to improvise a conversation as in the whole-class phase. Then record some of the dialogue together, each writing the words of their character.

Differentiation

Low Attainers – record one exchange of dialogue in speech bubbles first, then rewrite as dialogue with your help.
High Attainers – set the dialogue within a simple narrative.

Plenary

Choose pairs of children to 'perform' the dialogue they have written. Work together to write it down, explaining and demonstrating conventions of punctuation.

Lesson 4

Whole class

Read an enlarged text extract with dialogue, preferably the continuation of that in the previous lesson. Prompt children to identify and discuss who is speaking, and what they can tell about his/her feelings and relationships from the way he/she talks. Develop the commentaries and evaluations of characters from Lesson 2.

Read through the text until you reach the first word used to set up the dialogue, *e.g. said, asked.* Explain the function of these words, and ask children to write down others in the extract. Share and compile a list. Brainstorm others and add to the list. Choose children to say something in the way suggested by these words. Highlight the first contracted form – *e.g. you're* – in the extract, and ask children what they notice. Identify the two words joined and the placing of the apostrophe to indicate where letters have been omitted. Give children time-out to record other examples used in this and other extracts of dialogue read in the unit. Share, and compile a list.

Group and independent work

Display a list of common dialogue words; ask children to write appropriate exchanges of dialogue using each of them and including some contracted forms.

Differentiation

Low Attainers – Copymaster 45: complete exchanges of dialogue illustrating a range of dialogue words.
High Attainers – Copymaster 46: write a conversation using less common dialogue words.

Plenary

Ask children to read the exchanges of dialogue they have written in a tone appropriate to the dialogue word. Identify and spell the contracted forms used.

Lesson 5

Whole class

Draw together ideas about the behaviour of the characters in the shared text, revising and extending the lists of words to describe them. Suggest a new situation, *e.g. a character gets an expensive present or hurts him/herself.* Ask pairs of children to think about how the characters would behave and what they would say to each other. Share ideas, discussing whether they are consistent with what we know about the characters. Choose an idea to develop together, and use shared writing strategies to compose the opening of a new chapter or episode. As the writing proceeds, focus attention on the key teaching points from this unit:

- **pronouns:** Shall we use the name or a pronoun here? Which pronoun?
- **dialogue words:** What word could we use instead of 'said'?
- **punctuation of dialogue**: Give children time-out occasionally to write what two characters might say next; indicate where letters have been omitted. Give children time-out to record other examples used in this and other extracts of dialogue read in the unit. Share, and compile a list.

- **contracted forms:** Where does the apostrophe go here?

Group and independent work

Children write an episode – including dialogue – based on the story read in whole-class work or one read independently. Encourage them to choose a simple story-line with only one or two events.
This provides an opportunity for more extended writing in other Literacy Hours.

Differentiation

Low Attainers – continue and complete the episode begun in whole-class work.
High Attainers – encourage children to focus on depiction of character and use of dialogue.

Plenary

Share work in progress, looking for opportunities to reinforce and extend the teaching points, and to encourage children to try them out in their own writing.

Theme 5) Extended story

Objectives

Text level:
- 2 refer to significant aspects of the text
- 5 discuss a character's feelings, behaviour and relationships
- 10 plot a sequence of episodes as a plan for writing
- 13 write more extended stories, set out in chapters and organised in paragraphs

Sentence level:
- 4 use speech marks and other dialogue punctuation
- 5 recognise how sentences can be joined in more complex ways
- 6 investigate how words and phrases signal time

Resources

A familiar adventure story to serve as the 'core' story and 'model' in this unit. Enlarged text extracts from this story illustrating description of setting and character, plot development and creation of suspense. A variety of story books that provide information about their authors.
Copymasters 49 & 50. Homework 25.

Assessment

At the end of this theme is the pupil able to:
- plan incidents for a more extended story, organising them in chapters;
- establish coherence by linking sentences and organising them in paragraphs;
- use words that signal time – to indicate the sequence of events clearly;
- include description of character and setting as an element of story writing;
- use dialogue as an element in story writing, and begin to arrange and punctuate it accurately?

Lesson 1

Whole class

Prompt children to retell the main events of an adventure story they have recently read or listened to. Identify the most exciting moments and turning points, and discuss what makes a story an adventure.
Explain that in these lessons they will be writing their own adventure story.
Outline and write up the four-part generic framework for an adventure story as set out on Copymaster 49. Together discuss one or two possibilities for stories with this framework, including ones linked to reading.
Give pairs of children time out to develop other ideas. Share and discuss, and choose a story-line to develop together. Record this in broad terms in the four sections of the framework.
Explain that their story will have four chapters, corresponding to the four parts of the framework. Plan the sequence of events for the first chapter in more detail,

e.g. as a list of numbered or bulleted points. Ask children to think of a title for this chapter and write it down. Share ideas, and agree on the title that works best.

Group and independent work
Children use Copymaster 49 to plan an adventure story of their own that follows the framework. They then plan the sequence of events for the first chapter, and give this a title.

Differentiation
Low Attainers – encourage and help children to adapt and develop the story plan from whole-class work.
High Attainers – encourage children to invent a storyline of their own.

Plenary
Choose children to share the title and plans for their first chapter. Prompt others to discuss this as the opening to an adventure. Does it make them want to read on? What do they think might happen next?

Lesson 2

Whole class

Read together an enlarged text extract from the 'core' story in which characters are described. Identify words and phrases in the text that tell the reader (directly or indirectly) about a character's appearance, feelings and personality. Highlight any that are adjectives, and revise the function of this word-class from Term 2.
Confirm the two child characters in the class story, and discuss what they might be like. How can we make them different? Will one of them be the main character?
Ask children to work together in pairs to write down words and phrases to describe one of these characters. Share ideas, and choose some to develop together.
Using shared writing techniques, draw on these ideas and the plan to draft the opening of the first chapter of the class story. Focus children's attention on character description and organising ideas in paragraphs, *e.g. an*

opening paragraph that describes the situation; then a paragraph about each of the children; then a paragraph or paragraphs about how they become separated from the adults they are with.

Group and independent work
Children write the first chapter of their own story, focusing in particular on character description.
If possible, arrange here and throughout the theme for children to have more time outside the Literacy Hour to work on each chapter.

Differentiation
Low Attainers – show children where to include one or two sentences describing each character.
High Attainers – ask children to describe how the characters behave and feel.

Plenary
Share character descriptions. Highlight and discuss words that describe appearance and behaviour vividly.

Lesson 3

Whole class

Read together an enlarged text extract from the 'core' story in which setting and atmosphere are described. Identify relevant words and phrases in the text, and discuss the impact they have and the image that they evoke for the reader.

Remind the children that in the second chapter of their story the two children will move or be taken to a new place. List and discuss the places where adventures conventionally happen in stories and where they might happen. Choose a place that fits the opening situation of the class story and ask children, working in pairs, to list words and phrases to describe it.

Share these, identifying and listing ones which are powerful and atmospheric.

Use shared writing techniques to draft the opening of the second chapter of the class story. As before, focus on the organisation of ideas in paragraphs, and draw on the list of words to describe the new setting.

Group and independent work

Children plan and write the second chapter of their story, focusing on how the children get to the new place and describing it.

Differentiation

Low Attainers – help children to compile a small bank of words they could use in their description.

High Attainers – challenge children to create an atmosphere of mystery or danger.

Plenary

Choose children to read their descriptions of settings. Ask others to think of words that could be used to describe it more vividly and to create atmosphere.

Lesson 4

Whole class

Recap the class story so far. Ask children to imagine how the characters would react to being separated and in a mysterious or dangerous place. What would they say to each other? Ask pairs of children to develop a short conversation; more able writers could write this down.

Share ideas, and choose some to develop together. Use shared writing techniques to draft the dialogue. Revise conventions for the punctuation of dialogue and how it is organised in paragraphs.

Explain that they have now reached the point in the adventure where something exciting happens. Read together an enlarged text extract of the crisis point in the 'core' story. Explain how the author creates suspense, *e.g. by holding back information.*

Discuss what the exciting, dangerous event might be in the class story, *e.g. getting trapped, encountering someone* who is or who appears to be mysterious or threatening. Choose one, and draft this episode together. Focus attention on creating suspense and using words that signal time, *e.g. suddenly, just then, meanwhile.*

Group and independent work

Children plan and draft the third chapter of their story, incorporating some dialogue between the two children in it.

Differentiation

Low Attainers – record the conversation as a sequence of speech bubbles inserted in the main narrative.

High Attainers – challenge children to write a more extended conversation, with conventional punctuation and layout.

Plenary

Organise pairs of children to perform the conversations as a 'play'.

Share some of the 'crisis points'; discuss how they could be made more exciting.

Lesson 5

Whole class

Retell the crisis of the class story, and ask: *What happens now? How will the story end?* Identify and list possibilities, *e.g. for rescue or revelation.* Discuss which brings the story to the most satisfying conclusion. Use shared writing techniques to compose the episode in which the crisis is resolved. Again, draw attention to words that signal time, *e.g. after a while, soon.* Explain how they link sentences and offer alternatives to 'and' and 'then'.

Explain that they will soon be finishing their own stories – and are authors! Distribute books to pairs of children and ask them to find and read the information about their authors. Share this, and identify the kinds of information included (see Copymaster 50). Investigate how and where this information is presented. Choose one child in the class (or yourself), and draft a short author profile together.

Group and independent work

Children plan and write the final chapter of their story. Write titles for any untitled chapters and the story as a whole. Children write a profile of themselves as author. They then design a front and back cover for their story, including this profile and a picture of themselves. This work will need to be continued in other Literacy Hours and/or outside this context.

Differentiation

Low Attainers – Copymaster 50: make notes about themselves for an author profile.

High Attainers – Copymaster 50: in addition, write a 'blurb' for their adventure story.

Plenary

Share and discuss author profiles.

Discuss and plan ways of presenting their stories in a finished form for other children to read.

Theme 6 First and third person narratives

Objectives

Text level:
- 2 refer to significant aspects of the text
- 3 distinguish between first and third person accounts
- 4 consider credibility of events in stories
- 11 write openings to stories linked to reading
- 12 write a first person account

Sentence level:
- 2 identify pronouns and understand their function
- 3 ensure grammatical agreement

Word level:
- 11 use the apostrophe to spell shortened forms

Resources

A collection of adventure novels and short stories told in the first and third persons. Enlarged text extracts from a selection of these, focusing on passages in which suspense is built up or atmosphere evoked.
Copymasters 51 & 52. Homework 26.

Assessment

At the end of this theme is the pupil able to:
- distinguish between stories told in the first and third persons;
- discuss how effects – especially suspense and atmosphere – are created, referring to the detail of the text;
- write first and third person stories, using these 'voices' consistently;
- rewrite a third person account in the first person;
- identify pronouns in a text, and understand which nouns they refer to;
- write sentences in which subject and verb 'agree', and identify errors in agreement;
- spell shortened forms of words, placing the apostrophe accurately?

Lesson 1

Whole class

Read to the children an enlarged text extract from an adventure story told in the first person. (If it is not the opening of the story, recap events which lead up to this point.) Re-read it, prompting children to join in.
Give children, working in pairs, time-out to formulate three ideas about the extract and how it is written. Share these ideas. As the discussion develops, focus children's attention on the kind of story it is, and how they can tell: suspense and atmosphere, and how these effects are created. Encourage children to refer to the detail of the text, and highlight relevant words and phrases.
Ask: *Who is telling the story? How do you know?* Draw out the idea that the narrator is a character in the story. Identify and highlight words (pronouns) that indicate this and sentences in which his/her involvement in the action is clear. Ask children to suggest other stories written in this way. Have examples from the collection ready to share.

Group and independent work

Ask each group to find another story in the class collection which is told in the first person, and be ready to read a sentence which makes this clear.
Children write a short account in the first person of an adventure that really happened to them.

Differentiation

Low Attainers – Copymaster 51: read and distinguish between short extracts from first-and third-person stories.
High Attainers – in addition, write a 'label' explaining who the narrator is and his/her role in the story.

Plenary

Choose children to read a few sentences from the first-person story they have found.
Choose children to read their real-life adventure.
In both cases, discuss the question: *How do we know who is telling the story?*

Lesson 2

Whole class

Display an extract from a more challenging adventure story told in the third person. Ask children to read it aloud, taking a couple of sentences each. Look for opportunities to reinforce and extend strategies for reading and working out the meaning of unfamiliar words. Display the extract read in Lesson 1. Give pairs of children time-out to re-read this, and to compare the two extracts, finding two differences and two similarities. Share ideas. Encourage children to refer to the detail of the text, and highlight significant words and phrases.
Ask: *Who is telling this story? How do we know?* Confirm that the story is told not by a character taking part in the events but as if by someone observing events from the 'outside'. Identify and highlight words that indicate this.

Ask children to suggest other stories written in this way, and share some examples from the collection.

Group and independent work

Ask each group to find a story told in the third person, and be ready to read a sentence which makes this clear. Rewrite the real-life adventure from Lesson 1 in the third person.

Differentiation

Low Attainers – make and label a small display of picture-book stories told in the first and third persons.
High Attainers – scan a collection of short stories; identify ones told in first/third person.

Plenary

Choose children to read sentences from their third person story. Discuss: *How do we know who's telling the story?*
Display a first person adventure from Lesson 1 and work together to retell it in the third person.

Lesson 3

Whole class

Write up a pair of sentences in the second of which nouns from the first are replaced by pronouns. Highlight the pronouns in the second sentence and ask children what they refer to. Draw lines linking them back to the corresponding nouns. Repeat.

Introduce and explain the term 'pronoun'. Write up examples from these sentences, and prompt children to suggest others to add to the list.

Return to the enlarged text from Lesson 1 or 2. Find the first three pronouns together, and identify the nouns to which they refer. Ask children to divide a piece of paper into two columns, and record every pronoun in the text and its related noun. Work through the text together, checking this.

Select from the text (and/or provide) examples of shortened forms in which pronouns and verbs are joined e.g. *I'll, they're*. Explain how the apostrophe is used where letters are omitted. Prompt children to suggest other examples and write them up in full and short forms.

Group and independent work

Identify and list the first ten pronouns in a story. Write full versions of any short forms used.

Write up sentences with nouns and ask children to write a follow-up sentence for each using pronouns. (Alternatively, present this as a worksheet.)

Differentiation

Low Attainers – Copymaster 52: fill gaps in the sentences with the right pronoun.

High Attainers – write a short description without using pronouns; rewrite it, using pronouns.

Plenary

Work together to compose descriptions of something without and with pronouns.

Identify places where short/full forms could be used; spell the short forms.

Lesson 4

Whole class

Prepare for this lesson by writing up sentences in which subject pronouns and verbs are not in grammatical agreement, *e.g. They was ..., I is ...* Prompt children to identify and correct the errors. Draw out the general idea that pronouns and verbs need to 'match'.

Choose a regular verb – *e.g. to look* – and work through all the subject pronoun combinations – *I look, he looks ...* – noting where the verb form changes. Ask children to repeat this on paper for another regular verb. Share and check.

Explain that this is not always straightforward, and work through the pronouns for an irregular verb, *e.g. to be, to go*.

Choose a familiar traditional story and a character in it. Ask children to imagine that this character is telling the story. Use shared writing techniques to write the first few sentences, focusing on pronouns and grammatical agreement. Give pairs of children time-out to write the next few sentences. Share and check.

Group and independent work

Children retell an episode from another traditional story in the first person from the point of view of one of the characters.

Differentiation

Low Attainers – provide the first few sentences to establish the 'voice'.

High Attainers – write a version of *Cinderella* told by the Ugly Sisters, using plural pronouns – *we, our, us*.

Plenary

Choose a child to take on the role of a character in a traditional story; prompt others to ask him/her questions about what happens in the story. Write up responses in the first person, drawing attention – where appropriate – to pronouns and agreement.

Lesson 5

Whole class

Present an adventure story scenario, focusing on a moment of uncertainty, *e.g. entering a ruined house in search of someone, clambering on to a roof as floodwaters rise*. Give children time-out to develop a storyline based on this. Share; choose one to work on together.

Decide together on whether the story will be told in the first or third person.

Ask individuals or pairs to write the first few sentences of the story. Encourage them to create an atmosphere of excitement or danger.

Share some opening sentences. Discuss their effectiveness.

Using shared writing techniques, draw on these contributions to compose a story opening. Focus on using pronouns consistently to establish a first or third person voice, and on choice of detail and words to create atmosphere and suspense.

Group and independent work

Children write the opening of their own adventure story in the first or third person, based on one read in this unit or on the real-life adventure they wrote in Lesson 1. Though short, this task offers an opportunity for more extended writing in subsequent Literacy Hours and/or outside this context.

Differentiation

Low Attainers – write another story opening for the scenario set up in this lesson.

High Attainers – encourage children to focus on atmosphere and suspense.

Plenary

Choose samples of work in progress to share and discuss, looking for opportunities to reinforce and extend teaching points covered in the unit.

Theme 7) Humorous poetry and language play

Objectives

Text level:
- 2 refer to significant aspects of a text
- 6 compare forms or types of humour
- 7 select, prepare, read aloud and recite poetry that plays with language or entertains

Sentence level:
- 1 use awareness of grammar to decipher new or unfamiliar words

Word level:
- 8 identify short words within longer words
- 12 collect new words from reading
- 14 explore homonyms

Resources
Enlarged text versions of humorous poems of the kinds identified in the lessons below, e.g. nonsense poems by Edward Lear and Spike Milligan; cautionary tales by Hillaire Belloc, Ogden Nash and Shel Silverstein, and of poems that play with language, e.g. acrostics, puns.
Anthologies of humorous and nonsense verse at appropriate levels. Joke books.
Copymasters 53 & 54. Homework 27.

Assessment
At the end of this theme is the pupil able to:
- identify and discuss different kinds of humorous poetry and language play;
- use a range of reading strategies to work out unfamiliar words;
- read aloud and recite poems using expression and intonation to bring out the effects;
- understand that some words have multiple meanings, and use context to distinguish these;
- experiment and play with language to create simple poems and word play texts?

Lesson 1

Whole class

Read an enlarged text copy of a humorous poem to the children while they follow the text. Give them time to re-read it independently and silently, and then invite ideas and responses. As the discussion develops, prompt children to focus on what makes the poem funny, considering both the content and use of words.
Display an enlarged text copy of a contrasting and more challenging humorous poem, and ask the children to read it to you, e.g. taking a line or verse each. When they hesitate or make a mistake, prompt them to use a range of strategies to work out or confirm words.
Identify, list and discuss the meaning of words that are unusual and/or interesting.
Ask children to work in pairs to compare the two poems. Share ideas, alternating between differences and similarities. Focus attention on what makes the text funny and on significant aspects of language and structure.

Group and independent work
Give each group copies of two or three humorous poems at an appropriate reading level. Ask children to read them; to choose a favourite; to note down new and/or interesting words; and to prepare a group reading-aloud performance.

Differentiation
Low Attainers – listen to recordings of the poems, then read them.
High Attainers – use a dictionary to discover or check the meaning of words.

Plenary
Choose children to read their poem aloud. Identify ways in which this could be improved to bring out the humour, and re-read with them.
Pool new and interesting words, discussing their meanings. Make a class list.

Lesson 2

Whole class

Display an enlarged text copy of an acrostic poem. Ask children to read it independently and silently. Then share reading as in Lesson 1; prompt use of strategies to read new words; work out and discuss the meaning of any unusual words.
Ask children what they notice about the structure of the poem; draw out the idea that the first letters of each line make a word. Identify and write up this word.
Introduce the term 'acrostic' to describe poetry and word puzzles of this type.
Write up another short word vertically; use shared writing techniques to compose lines for an acrostic poem. Prompt children to search their vocabularies for interesting and powerful words. Give pairs of children time-out to write some lines independently; share, develop, and add chosen lines to the poem.

Display the text of a poem that plays with language in a different way (see Copymasters 53 and 54 for two possibilities). Read together; identify and discuss how the word play works. Experiment with writing other examples.

Group and independent work
Children write an acrostic poem about themselves using the letters of their first name.

Differentiation
Low Attainers – Copymaster 53: read a poem which plays with different meanings of the same word; write new lines modelled on this structure.
High Attainers – Copymaster 54: read a poem based on finding words within words; use this kind of word play to write new lines.

Plenary
Choose children to share their word play poems.
Discuss how they work; write up relevant words; invent new examples together.

Lesson 3

Whole class

Write up and read the traditional rhyme 'Dr Bell': *Dr Bell fell down a well/And broke his collar bone./Doctors should attend the sick/And leave the well alone.* Ask children to find the joke. Draw out the idea that it depends on the fact that the word 'well' has two meanings, and explain that lots of jokes work like this. Introduce the term 'pun' to describe this kind of word play.

Tell jokes of this kind, and ask the children to identify the word that has two meanings and what they are.

Write up a pair of sentences including homonyms, *e.g. club, chip,* used in different senses. Read these together and explain that the meanings can be worked out from the context.

Write up examples of other homonyms and ask children to identify the different meanings. Choose some, and ask children to write sentences including them. Share and check meanings.

Group and independent work

Look in joke books to find examples of jokes that depend on puns. Choose a favourite to share.

Write a list of other homonym pairs; choose one, and write sentences to show the different meanings.

Differentiation

Low Attainers – provide a list of common homonyms for children to use in sentences.

High Attainers – challenge children to find words with more than two meanings, and write sentences illustrating them. They could look in a dictionary for ideas.

Plenary

Share favourite jokes; identify the pun and its two meanings.

Compile a class list of homonyms, and identify their various meanings.

Lesson 4

Whole class

Display an enlarged text copy of a cautionary tale. Read the first verse to the children; ask them to read the rest out loud, *e.g. a line or couplet at a time.* Model use of a range of strategies to read new words; work out and discuss the meaning of any unusual words. Prompt children to retell the story in their own words, sharing episodes round the class. Identify and discuss the main idea and purpose of the poem: What moral is it supposed to teach?

Re-read the poem. Ask children what they notice about its style and structure; highlight and discuss relevant features, *e.g. pattern of rhyme, organisation of verses.* Explain that poems like this are usually intended to warn children about the consequences of bad behaviour, but that they are going to write one that warns adults. Discuss possibilities for this, *e.g. smoking, lack of exercise,*

working too hard, and choose one. Give pairs of children time-out to develop a story line, focusing on the gruesome, exaggerated consequences.

Share ideas; choose one, and used shared writing techniques to compose the beginning of a cautionary tale in prose.

Group and independent work

Plan and write a cautionary tale of their own in prose.

Differentiation

Low Attainers – continue and complete the cautionary tale begun in whole-class work.

High Attainers – focus on describing the consequences in humorous detail.

Plenary

Choose children to share their cautionary tales.

Read the beginning of another cautionary tale in verse; pause for children to predict the outcome, and read on.

Lesson 5

Whole class

Display an enlarged text copy of a narrative nonsense poem. Read the first verse to the children. As in Lesson 4, ask them to read the rest out loud, and work on new words and meanings.

Prompt children to share responses and ideas freely. As the discussion develops, focus attention on aspects of the story that are 'impossible', and highlight these in the text. Introduce and explain the term 'nonsense verse' to describe poetry of this kind.

Ask pairs of children to think of other impossible things that they could make happen in a story. Share ideas. Choose one, and use shared writing techniques to write a short episode together.

Write up and read the first verse of H. E. Wilkinson's poem Topsy-Turvy Land: *The people walk upon their heads,/The sea is made of sand,/The children go to school by night,/In Topsy-*

Turvy Land. Explain that the nonsense here depends on reversing things. Give the children time-out to think of other reversals; record some in short sentences, as in the poem.

Group and independent work

Write a short nonsense story, basing it on the poem read in whole-class work or using ideas of their own.

Write sentences, modelled on those in *Topsy-Turvy Land,* to state other reversals.

Differentiation

Low Attainers – give children sentence starters for reversals, *e.g. People swim ..., Bald men ...*

High Attainers – write verses modelled on that from *Topsy-Turvy Land.*

Plenary

Share and discuss nonsense stories and reversals.

Review the different kinds of humorous poetry and word play read and written during the unit. Discuss preferences and reasons for these.

Theme 9) Poetry that uses sound

Objectives

Text level:
- 2 refer to significant aspects of the text
- 7 recognise rhyme, alliteration and other patterns of sound
- 15 write poetry that uses sound to create effects

Word level:
- 1 revise spelling of words with long vowel phonemes
- 2 identify, blend and segment phonemes
- 6 use independent spelling strategies: sounding out and spelling using phonemes; spelling by analogy

Resources
Enlarged text copies of poems that use sound in the ways highlighted in the lessons below. Examples of poems with distinct rhythms for Lesson 4 include James Reeves' *Cows* (slow), David McCord's *Song of the Train* or Clive Sansom's *The Train Goes Running Along the Line* (both quick and jerky).
Anthologies of poetry at appropriate reading levels.

Assessment
At the end of this theme is the pupil able to:
- identify and discuss ways in which sound is used in poetry and the different effects this creates;
- analyse and discuss patterns of sound in a poem;
- experiment with sound patterns to write their poems, modelled on examples read;
- sound out and spell words using knowledge of phonemes;
- show understanding of the different ways in which the same phoneme can be spelled?

Lesson 1

Whole class

In this theme the children will be exploring how poets use the sounds of words.
Write up a few onomatopoeic words, *e.g. pop, splash, whoosh, sizzle.* Ask children to read them, and ask: *What do you notice?* Draw out the general idea that the sounds of these words are like the sounds of the things or actions they stand for. Introduce the term 'onomatopoeia' to describe this.
Suggest a subject which involves different noisy activities, *e.g. cooking, or animal movements and sounds.* Ask children, working together in pairs, to list onomatopoeic words that describe these activities. Share and write up words, and read them together.
Use these words to revise spelling patterns for:
- initial consonant clusters, especially *sp, sl, fl, sn;*
- doubled letters in the middle and at the end of words, especially *zz, ss* and *tt;*
- final consonant clusters, especially *sh, ch* and *ng.* Generate and list other words that follow these patterns, giving children time-out to list some.

Group and independent work
Write up other areas of activity, *e.g. movement of and in water, movement of different vehicles,* and ask children to list onomatopoeic words to describe them.

Differentiation
Low Attainers – Copymaster 57: write an appropriate onomatopoeic word to describe the actions/noises shown in the series of pictures.
High Attainers – invent and spell new onomatopoeic words.

Plenary
Choose children to say an onomatopoeic word; ask others to say what action it describes.
Pool onomatopoeic words; sort them according to spelling patterns, as in whole-class work.
Ask children to share new onomatopoeic words, and add them to the lists.

Lesson 2

Whole class

Say a tongue twister to the class. Challenge individuals to repeat it. How fast can they go without getting into a muddle? Try with another.
Ask children why it is difficult to say them quickly and clearly. Write up the tongue twisters, and identify and highlight repeated sounds or shifts between sounds. Identify the spelling patterns, and ask children to list other words with the same patterns on their whiteboards. Draw on these lists to write new tongue twisters.
Read together an enlarged text copy of a poem which uses alliteration. Ask the children what they notice, and identify and highlight strings of words beginning with the same sound. Introduce the term 'alliteration' to describe this. Discuss the effect, *e.g. fun and/or vivid, description.*
Write up couplets from an alliterative ABC, *e.g. Angry Arnold tore his coat/Boastful Bobby sailed his boat,* or counting rhyme, *e.g. Ten tiny turtles, walking on the sand/Nine naughty nightingales coming in to land.* Use shared writing techniques to write other lines. Look for opportunities to draw attention to different ways of spelling the same consonant phoneme.

Group and independent work
Write their own tongue twisters, and practise saying them.
Write other lines for the alliterative ABC or counting rhyme.

Differentiation
Low Attainers – write adjective and noun pairings for each letter of the alphabet.
High Attainers – write in rhyming couplets.

Plenary
Choose children to say their tongue twister. Challenge others to say it fast.
Share alliterative lines and couplets. Ask children if they have found different ways of spelling the same consonant phoneme; list; add other examples.

Lesson 3

Whole class

Prepare an enlarged copy of a simple rhyming poem by covering the second word of each pair. Read the poem together, pausing for children to identify the 'missing' words. Revise the term 'rhyme', and highlight all the rhyming words. Ask children to work out the pattern of rhyming words from verse to verse. Confirm and explain this. Repeat this process for a poem with a different rhyme scheme, this time covering up more of the rhyming words, including some which begin pairs or sets. Write lists of the rhyming words in these poems. Ask pairs of children to write more words for each list. Share, and compile class lists. Check spellings and underline the parts of words that rhyme. Look for opportunities to explain different ways of spelling the same vowel phoneme, and sort words in some lists according to these patterns.

Group and independent work

Give children a few minutes to find a rhyming poem in an anthology. Ask them to list all the rhyming words in pairs or sets, and to add more words to each list. Prepare to read their poem aloud to the rest of the class.

Differentiation

Low Attainers – give children a poem which uses common rhymes.
High Attainers – Copymaster 58: in addition, work out and describe the pattern of rhyme in their chosen poem.

Plenary

Choose children to introduce and read their poem, and to write up lists of the rhyming words; ask others to add more words to each list. As before, note different spelling patterns.

Lesson 4

Whole class

Read together an enlarged text copy of a poem with a slow, regular rhythm that reflects its subject. Ask children what they notice about the sounds of this poem; explain that the poet uses speed and rhythm to describe things. Note the use of words with long vowel phonemes. Ask children to write 'slow' words. Share, and compile a list. As before, identify different ways of spelling the same phoneme. Draw on these words to write a sentence or phrase that describes something slow or calm. Then ask children to try this independently. Share and write up contributions.
Repeat this teaching sequence for a poem with a quick, jerky rhythm. In this case, focus on the spelling of words with a succession of short vowel phonemes and hard-sounding consonants.

Group and independent work

Write sentences that use sound and rhythm to describe things that move quickly and slowly.
Choose (from a selection) a rhythmic poem; prepare and rehearse a group reading performance.

Differentiation

Low Attainers – prepare a reading of one of the poems from the whole-class phase.
High Attainers – write a sequence of lines with the same rhythmic pattern.

Plenary

Choose children to read their poem to the rest of the class; identify and discuss how rhythm is used.
Share descriptions of fast/slow things. Write up and check spelling of key words. (Keep these for the next lesson.)

Lesson 5

Whole class

Choose something that moves quickly or slowly and makes noises, *e.g. an animal or vehicle*. Recap work done on onomatopoeia and alliteration. Ask children to list words and strings of words that could be used to describe the chosen subject by representing associated sounds. Share and record contributions.
Recap work done on rhythm. Discuss whether 'quick' or 'fast' words and rhythms would be right for describing the chosen subject. Ask children to write words and phrases with the appropriate quality. Share and record these. Using shared writing techniques, draw on this word bank to compose the first line of a poem. Pause, and prompt children to think about what might come next. If appropriate, encourage them to think of a line that would rhyme with and/or continue the rhythm of the first. Alternatively, create a poem with a looser structure.

Pause occasionally to read and re-read the poem; prompt children to think of ways of improving it.

Group and independent work

Children choose another noisy, fast/slow thing; compile a bank of sound words to describe it, and draw on this to write a poem.

Differentiation

Low Attainers – write a poem with a simple list-like structure, *e.g. each line beginning with the name of the subject.*
High Attainers – write patterned verses.

Plenary

Choose children to read their poems, or do this for them. Identify and discuss sound effects.
Discuss and plan the compilation of a class collection of sound poems.

Theme 10 Author study

Objectives

Text level:
- 1 retell, compare and evaluate stories
- 2 refer to significant aspects of the text
- 8 compare and contrast works by the same author
- 9 be aware of authors and discuss preferences
- 10 plot a sequence of episodes as a plan for writing
- 11 write openings linked to reading
- 14 write book reviews for a specified audience

Sentence level:
- 5 understand how sentences can be joined in more sophisticated ways
- 6 investigate how words and phrases signal time

Word level:
- 7 practise new spellings
- 12 collect new words from reading

Resources

A range of books by the chosen author for this unit; enlarged text extracts from a selection of these books, representing variety within this author's work, and including extracts that illustrate use of 'time' words to link sentences.

Collections of novels, short stories and picture books by other authors – enough for each group to focus on an author during independent work in this unit.

An enlarged text book review – written by yourself or a child.

Copymasters 59 & 60. Homework 30.

Assessment

At the end of this theme is the pupil able to:
- understand the idea of authorship, and gain information about specific authors from book covers, etc;
- identify and discuss characteristics of an author's work;
- express opinions about an author and justify them with reference to the text;
- plan and write a story episode modelled on the work of a particular author;
- identify and understand the function of words that signal time;
- use a wider range of these words in own writing, and spell them accurately?

Lesson 1

Whole class

Give children time-out to choose, from the class collection, a book by a favourite author. Ask them to write the titles of other books he/she has written and two things they like about them. Briefly share authors and ideas, and explain that in this unit they will be investigating authors and their work.

Show and talk through the selection of books by the core author. Establish whether the author is also the illustrator; if not, identify who the illustrator is. Ask children where they can find the author's name and information about him or her, *e.g. lists of other books published, biographical information*. Locate this information, and read it to the children.

Ask children to look for this information on their chosen book. Share and read some examples.

Group and independent work

For work in this unit, each group studies an author whose work they know and enjoy. Ask children to organise a small display of books by this author and compile a list of titles. They read autobiographical information, and note key facts. Some could use the internet to find this information.

Differentiation

Low Attainers – Copymaster 59: record information about the author.
High Attainers – organise the books in categories; write an explanatory label for each type.

Plenary

Choose groups to present their displays of books, and to share what they found out about their author. Ask questions which focus attention on key points: Where did you find this information? Is she/he the illustrator too? Does she/he write different kinds of books?

Lesson 2

Whole class

Choose and introduce two books by the 'core' author which have marked similarities. Read an enlarged text extract from one of these to the children; then display another, and ask them to read to you.

Ask pairs to identify and record similarities between the two extracts. Share ideas considering character, setting, theme, tone. Then ask children if they notice any similarities in how the stories are written. Identify and discuss features of style. Prompt children to make statements about the author's work (rather than specific books) and to refer to the text.

Return to one of the episodes, and ask children to identify the main events and list them.

Identify and highlight words in the text which indicate the sequence of events in time, and explain their function.

Group and independent work

Ask individuals or pairs to read the beginning of two books by their author, and then to identify and discuss what they have in common. Write a list of similarities.

Differentiation

Low Attainers – write a sentence under headings for setting, characters, ideas.
High Attainers – encourage children to consider how the stories are told as well as content.

Plenary

Choose children to introduce the books by their author to the rest of the class, identifying common features, and illustrating them from the text, *e.g. by reading opening sentences*.

Lesson 3

Whole class

Read an enlarged text extract from a story which contrasts markedly with those discussed in Lesson 2. Do you think this is by ('core' author)? Why? Why not? Prompt children to identify similarities and differences in characters, settings, theme, tone and style. Record these in two columns.

Re-read the extract, and identify the main events in the sequence. Highlight words that indicate time. Explain how these are used to link sentences. Write up a list of time words; add others identified in Lesson 2.

Choose two or three of the words, and ask children to write sentences or pairs of sentences including them. Share, and write up examples that illustrate the function of these words clearly.

Identify significant aspects of spelling, and practise using the 'look, say, cover, write, check' method.

Group and independent work

Ask each child in the group to read a story by their author, and to note 'time words'; share and compile a group list. Then use Copymaster 60 to complete sentences including time words.

Differentiation

Low Attainers – write sentences about the school day, beginning with given (simpler) time words, *e.g. first, when, then, next.*

High Attainers – write sentences linked by or including each of the time words they have found (supplement with others if necessary).

Plenary

Ask children if they have found any time words not included on the class list; confirm, and use in sentences. Take other time words in turn, and ask children to contribute sentences including them.

Lesson 4

Whole class

Read together the enlarged text book review. Ask children what kind of writing this is, and introduce and explain the term 'book review'. Identify the different kinds of information it provides and points at which the author expresses an opinion about the book.

Choose a book by the 'core' author with which the children are familiar from Lessons 1–3. Display the enlarged text extract(s) and, if possible, make copies available to groups. Ask groups to share ideas about what they like or don't like about this book and why; ask them to choose one idea, and to write a sentence expressing it.

Drawing on these ideas, use shared writing techniques to plan a book review, *e.g. in terms of different elements such as theme, characters, setting, appeal.*

Work together to begin drafting a review. Focus on giving reasons for likes and dislikes, prompting children to refer to the text.

Discuss purpose of book reviews in informing people about books they might not know; identify possible audiences.

Group and independent work

Ask individual children to choose one of the audiences, and plan and write a short review of one of the books by their 'core' author.

Differentiation

Low Attainers – write three pairs of sentences with the structure *I like ..., I like this because ...*

High Attainers – include information about the general characteristics of the author's work.

Plenary

Choose children to read their reviews; prompt them to comment on key points, especially whether personal opinions have been explained and justified.

Lesson 5

Whole class

Return to the pair of related books discussed in Lesson 2. Revise features that link them. Discuss possibilities for another book in the series, *e.g. same characters in a different setting or situation, introducing a new character.*

Ask pairs of children to develop a story-line for a new book in the series; and to note main ideas.

Share ideas, and choose one to develop together. Record the main events in sequence as a plan for the story.

Use shared writing techniques to draft the opening episode. Draw attention to the style and mood of the original stories, and prompt children to use these features in this new story.

Pause to focus on use of time words to link sentences, prompting children to consider possibilities other than 'and' and 'then'.

Group and independent work

Children write the opening of a new story modelled on the linked books by their group's author. Alternatively, a group could plan a whole story together, and write an episode each. This provides an opportunity for more extended writing in other Literacy Hours and/or outside this context.

Differentiation

Low Attainers – help children to create a new story by making one or two changes to the original story.

High Attainers – encourage children to focus on the style and mood of their new story as well as similarities in content (drawing on work in Lesson 2).

Plenary

Choose children to read some or all of their new stories. Look for opportunities to discuss how the children's stories are linked with the series on which they are modelled. Also look together at their use of time words.

Dialogue

This is the beginning of Penny Dale's story *Bet You Can't!*
Use   full stops   •
or   question marks   ?
or   exclamation marks   !
to punctuate what the children say.

Now what are you doing

Hiding

Why

To get away from you

Well, I'll tidy up then

Bet you can't

Why

Because I'm in the basket

Let's both get in the basket

Bet we can't

Bet we can't
See   We can

What are you doing now

Tidying up

Write what the children say to each other next.

Dialogue

This is the beginning of David McPhail's story *Lost!*
Complete it by
• putting full stops, question marks or exclamation marks in the boxes
• writing a word for dialogue on the lines.

I am walking down the street when I hear someone crying ☐

It's a bear ☐

He looks lost and afraid ☐

The tall buildings scare him ☐

And he's never seen so many people ☐

"Don't worry," I _____

"The buildings won't hurt you, and most of the people are friendly ☐"

"How did you get here ☐" I _____ ☐

"I climbed in to get a nap," he _____, "and when I woke up,

I was lost ☐"

"I'll help you ☐ Tell me where you live ☐"

"There are trees where I live," he _____ ☐

So we find some trees ☐

"More trees," he _____, "and water ☐"

I take him to a place where there are more trees – and water, too ☐

"No," he says ☐ "This is not it either ☐"

I have an idea ☐

"Follow me ☐" I _____ ☐

Fiction and non-fiction

This is the beginning of William Steig's story *Doctor De Soto*.

Doctor De Soto, the dentist, did very good work, so he had <u>no end of</u> patients. Those close to his own size – moles, chipmunks, <u>et cetera</u> – sat in the regular dentist's chair.

Larger animals sat on the floor while Doctor De Soto stood on a ladder.

For extra-large animals, he had a special room. There Doctor De Soto was <u>hoisted</u> up to the patient's mouth by his assistant, who also happened to be his wife.

Doctor De Soto was especially popular with the big animals. He was able to work inside their mouths, wearing <u>galoshes</u> to keep his feet dry; and his fingers were so delicate, and his drill so <u>dainty</u>, they could hardly feel any pain.

Being a mouse, he refused to <u>treat</u> animals dangerous to mice, and it said so on his sign. When the doorbell rang, he and his wife would look out the window. They wouldn't <u>admit</u> even the most <u>timid-looking</u> cat.

One day, when they looked out, they saw a well-dressed fox with a <u>flannel</u> bandage around his jaw.

Work out the meaning of the underlined words and phrases.

no end of   _____

et cetera   _____

hoisted   _____

galoshes   _____

dainty   _____

treat   _____

admit   _____

timid-looking   _____

flannel   _____

Fiction and non-fiction

Choose an interesting double-page spread in a non-fiction book.
Put ticks in the column to show the ways in which information is
presented.

	√	notes about how they are used
headings		
pictures		
diagrams		
labels		
captions		
different text styles		
arrows		

Read the text. Write down any special or unusual words.

_____   _____   _____   _____

_____   _____   _____   _____

Non-chronological reports

The text and headings from this book about minibeasts have got muddled up.

Cut out the pieces and stick them down again in the right order.

You will see that there is no writing about one of the animals. Write some text yourself about this animal.

Minibeasts   (from *Minibeasts* by Angela Royston)

The bees carry the pollen back to the nest to feed the queen and her babies.

Snail

Spider

This spider makes a silk thread in its body. It uses the silk to spin a sticky web between plants. Then the spider sits and waits.

Bumblebee

When a fly gets caught in the web, the spider runs out and wraps it up in silk. It keeps the fly to eat later.

A ladybird lifts up its wing cases and spreads its wings to fly away.

Ladybird

Bumblebees live together in a nest in the ground. They work hard to look after the queen bee. The bees fly off to look for food. They sip juice from flowers and collect pollen on their hairy bodies.

A ladybird is a kind of beetle with colourful wing-cases.
The colour warns birds that ladybirds taste bad. Ladybirds eat greenfly which they find on plants.

Non-chronological reports

This piece of writing about wildlife in summer would be easier to understand if it were divided into sections with headings.

In the heat of summer, flowers bloom, insects multiply rapidly and fruits open. When the days are warm enough, summer flowers come into bloom. Compared with sturdy, low growing spring flowers, their stems are taller and their petals more delicate. Ladybirds are busy all summer eating aphids, such as greenfly, which breed in enormous numbers and suck the juice of plants. They lay their eggs on leaves. When the larvae hatch, they feed on aphids as well. Male grasshoppers and crickets sing all day long in the fields. Crickets sing by rubbing their wing sheaths together. Grasshoppers rub their hind legs against their wing-cases. In early summer, young frogs emerge from ponds. They live in damp places and feed at night on insects. Their skin can change colour to help them hide from snakes, rats and other enemies. Dragonflies are a common sight around ponds and riverbanks. They fly fast, hunting other small insects, such as gnats. They lay their eggs in water plants. The eggs hatch into nymphs, which live in the water for two years.

from *Summer* by Ruth Thomson

Write out the text again on a separate sheet of paper, organising it so that it has:
• a main heading
• a short introduction
• five sub-headings with text

Organisation and presentation of information

Here are some words for the index of a book about places.
Write them out in alphabetical order.

car park   _____

library   _____

building site   _____

museum   _____

fire station   _____

airport   _____

police station   _____

zoo   _____

market   _____

railway station   _____

farm   _____

school   _____

golf course   _____

park   _____

swimming pool   _____

windmill   _____

hospital   _____

Organisation and presentation of information

Imagine that you are the editor of a book about how everyday things are made and how they work.

These are the words for C and T in the index.

You need to sort them into alphabetical order.

| candle | clock | camera | chainsaw | chair | computer | car |

| caravan | crane | cup | coins | comb |

| tape recorder | television | telephone | teddy bear | toaster |

| trainers | toothbrush | thermometer | tractor | tram |

C _____

_____

_____

_____

_____

_____

_____

_____

_____

_____

_____

_____

T _____

_____

_____

_____

_____

_____

_____

_____

_____

_____

_____

_____

Playscripts

Reuben was taking a long time getting ready for school. And his
father was getting cross.
This is what they said to each other.

Come on, Reuben

I'm going as fast as I can
Where's your lunch box
it's still in the kitchen
Oh no
Shall I go and get it
No
It won't take long
No
Oh look
What
It was in my bag all the time
Are you ready
Yes

Finish each
sentence with:

a full stop   •

a question mark   ?

or an exclamation mark   !

Playscripts

This is the beginning of Jill Murphy's story *Whatever Next!*

Put the correct punctuation mark in each box.

"Can I go to the moon ☐ " asked Baby Bear.

"No you can't," said Mrs Bear ☐

"It's bathtime. Anyway, you'd have to find a rocket first ☐ "

Baby Bear found a rocket in the cupboard under the stairs ☐ He found a space-helmet on the draining board in the kitchen, and a pair of space-boots on the mat by the front door ☐

He packed his teddy and some food for the journey and took off up the chimney . . .

. . . WHOOSH ☐ Out into the night ☐

An owl flew past ☐

"That's a smart rocket," he said ☐ "Where are you off to ☐ "

"The moon," said Baby Bear ☐ "Would you like to come too ☐ "

"Yes please," said the owl ☐

Settings

Draw lines to link pairs of synonyms that describe similar places.

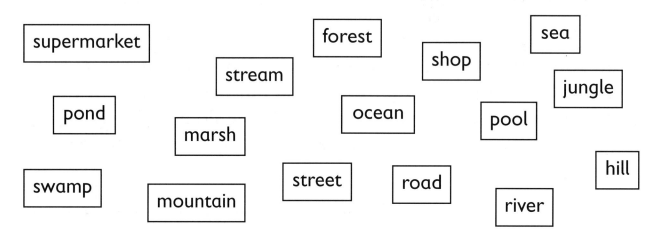

supermarket

stream

forest

shop

sea

jungle

pond

marsh

ocean

pool

swamp

street

road

river

mountain

hill

Write more words for places.

_____   _____   _____

_____   _____   _____

Draw lines to link sets of three synonyms that describe similar kinds of weather.

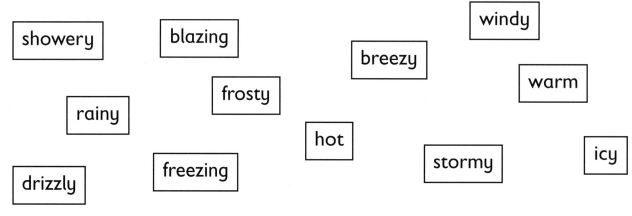

showery

blazing

windy

breezy

frosty

warm

rainy

hot

drizzly

freezing

stormy

icy

Write more words that describe the weather.

_____   _____   _____

_____   _____   _____

Settings

This is the beginning of Oscar Wilde's story *The Selfish Giant.*

Every afternoon, as they were coming from school, the children used to go and play in the Giant's garden.

It was a large lovely garden, with soft green grass. Here and there over the grass stood beautiful flowers like stars, and there were twelve peach-trees that in the spring-time broke out into delicate blossoms of pink and pearl, and in the autumn bore rich fruit. The birds sat on the trees and sang so sweetly that the children used to stop their games in order to listen to them. "How happy we are here!" they cried to each other.

Underline the words that describe the setting.

Find the words the author uses to describe

the grass   _____

the flowers   _____

the blossom   _____

the fruit   _____

the singing of the birds   _____

Draw a picture of the garden in spring.

Shape poems

Add *ing* to these words about moving fast.

hurry   _____

race   _____

run   _____

chase   _____

rush   _____

jog   _____

Use them to make a shape poem.

Shape poems

Look at and read this shape poem by Robert Froman.

HOT ENOUGH TO SEE

Why do the letters get smaller? _____

_____

Where do you start reading this poem? _____

_____

What shape do the words make? _____

_____

Why is the word 'shivers' in a different style? _____

_____

Thesauruses

Make these sentences more interesting by changing the words that are underlined.

1 Theo woke up and <u>got</u> out of bed.

_____

2 He <u>went</u> round the corner very fast.

_____

3 I had fish and chips for dinner. It was <u>nice</u>.

_____

4 Sue <u>got</u> some sweets at the shop.

_____

5 The book I am reading now is very <u>good</u>.

_____

6 I <u>put</u> the bricks into the wheelbarrow.

_____

Thesauruses

Here are some very common words. Write lists of words that you could use instead.

look

_____

_____

_____

_____

big

_____

_____

_____

_____

little

_____

_____

_____

_____

good

_____

_____

_____

_____

sad

_____

_____

_____

_____

like

_____

_____

_____

_____

say

_____

_____

_____

_____

run

_____

_____

_____

_____

hit

_____

_____

_____

_____

Choose a verb that fits in and makes sense in these sentences.

Verbs

1 My best friend is _____ Jake.

2 The hill was so steep I had to get off and _____ my bike.

3 I stayed in at play-time to _____ tidy up the classroom.

4 I _____ out the window and saw that it was snowing.

5 Frogs can _____ a long way.

6 I was _____ so fast I tripped up.

7 We can _____ the sound of the
sea from our house.

8 I _____ everywhere but I could not _____
my other sock.

9 I _____ Mum what the time was.

10 The workmen _____ a big hole in the road outside our
house.

Verbs

There are lots of mistakes with verbs in this piece of writing.
Find them, and write in the correct word above the mistake.

One summer evening a princess walk down to the woods. She was
playing with her golden ball. She throwed it up into the air and
catched it again and again. Then she droped it and it falled into a deep
pond.

The princess looked into the pond but it is so deep that she can not
see her ball. She beginned to cry.

While she were crying, a frog putted its head out of the water and
askt her what the matter is. The princess told the frog that she had
losted her golden ball.

The frog sayed that he would jumped into the pond and got her ball
back for her if the princess promise to marry him. The princess
promised, and the frog jump into the pond and swimmed down to the
bottom to get the golden ball. The princess wait and wait, and after a
while the frog comed up with the ball and give it to her.

The princess runned home as fast as she could. She never stoped to
thank the frog and soon she
forgot all about the promise she
had made.

Characters

Add the suffix *ful* or *less* to complete the words in these sentences.

1 You have to very care_____ when you pick up an egg or it will break.

2 I got into trouble for washing the floor but I was only trying to be help_____.

3 A broken pencil is use_____.

4 The care_____ driver bumped into the lamp post.

5 It is very peace_____ in the classroom when all the children have gone out to play.

6 Baby birds are help_____. Their parents have to feed them.

Write sentences of your own using these words.

1 _____

2 _____

3 _____

4 _____

5 _____

6 _____

Characters

Complete the columns by writing in the short or full form of the word. Make sure you put the apostrophe in the right place in the short forms.

FULL	SHORT
do not	
	I'm
	it's
	wouldn't
I will	
he is	
	we're
you are	
could not	
	they're
	that's

Write some more pairs of full and short forms.

Fables

Use this chart to make notes about a fable.

title _____	

characters   words to describe them

_____ { _____

_____

_____ { _____

_____

main events

moral

Fables

Choose one of these adjectives to fill the gaps in the sentences.

| crafty | greedy | sly | faithful | lazy | busy | helpless | tiny |

1 The _____ fox played a trick on the rabbit.

2 The _____ pig ate up all the food.

3 The _____ dog stayed by its owner.

4 The _____ wolf hid in the trees.

5 The _____ grasshopper had no food in the winter. But

the _____ ants had lots of food.

6 The _____ lion could not get out of the net. The

_____ mouse bit through the rope and set him free.

Add *ly* to these words, and use them to fill the gaps in the sentences.

| quick | noisy | careful |

1 The wolf ran as _____ as he could to Grandmother's house.

2 Baby Bear cried _____ when he saw that all his porridge
was gone.

3 The prince picked up the glass slipper _____.

93

Making notes

Write telegram messages from these characters in traditional stories.
REMEMBER: You have enough money for only ten words.

1 From Cinderella to her Fairy Godmother, explaining the situation and asking for help.

_____

_____

2 From one of the Ugly Sisters to the Prince, telling him that she lost a shoe at the ball last night and would like it back.

_____

_____

3 From Goldilocks to the Three Bears, apologising.

_____

_____

_____

_____

4 From the first Little Pig to the second Little Pig, warning of the danger from the Wolf.

_____

_____

Making notes

Here are descriptions of three creatures from outer space.

This is Zig. She has two eyes on the top of her head. She eats glass. She moves by floating over the ground. She has one long feeler. She communicates with flashing lights.

This is Mig. He has one eye in the middle of his face. He eats all kinds of metal. He moves on little wheels. He has two feelers. He communicates by making beeping noises.

This is Tig. She has four eyes in a row around her head. She eats plants. She moves by firing small jet engines. She has eight feelers. She communicates by moving her feelers.

Design a chart to record the information about these creatures.
Draw it below and fill it in.

Then invent another creature from outer space, and add information about it to the chart.

Myths and legends

Add *y* to these words and use them to fill the gaps in these sentences about a cat.

silk	dust	noise	sun

Remember the spelling rules for adding *y*!

Our cat has a lovely _____ coat.

Sometimes she rolls on the ground and gets _____.

She runs away if you are too _____.

She likes it when the weather is warm and _____.

PURR!

Myths and legends

Use this chart to help you plan your story.

Story planner for *How the* _____ *Became*

BEGINNING

What was the animal like to start with?

Where did it live then? How did it live?

What will change about its appearance?

MIDDLE

What happens to make it change?

Who else is in the story? What do they do?

END

How does it live now?

Performance poetry

Circle the commas in these sentences.
Practise reading the sentences so that they make good sense.

My favourite colours are pink, blue and purple.

Red bird, red bird, what do you see?

"Hello, Mum," said Bernard. "Not now, Bernard," said his mother.

Well, that wasn't Grace's idea of a father!

Next to her family, what Grace liked best was stories.

Claire had a bad knee, so she set off home to tell her mum all about it.

Mr Bear was tired, Mrs Bear was tired and Baby Bear was tired, so they all went to bed.

Once, oh small children round my knee, there were no stories on earth to hear.
All the stories belonged to Nyame, the Sky God. He kept them in a golden box next to his royal stool.

Then, one day, the old man went to pull up the turnip. He pulled and pulled again, but he could not pull it up. He called the old woman. The old woman pulled the old man, the old man pulled the turnip.

Look at all these clever cats,
Cats from Spain, Brazil and France,
Cats from Greece, Japan and Norway,
Cats who sing and fly and dance.

Performance poetry

Write down three words in each list.

words that rhyme with **go** – each with a different spelling pattern

_____   _____   _____

words that rhyme with **gate** – all with the same spelling pattern

_____   _____   _____

words that rhyme with **bird** – each with a different spelling pattern

_____   _____   _____

words that rhyme with **feet** – all with the same spelling pattern

_____   _____   _____

words that rhyme with **where** – all with a different spelling pattern

_____   _____   _____

words that rhyme with **fight** – all with the same spelling pattern

_____   _____   _____

words that rhyme with **door** – all with a different spelling pattern

_____   _____   _____

words that rhyme with **dear** – all with the same spelling pattern

_____   _____   _____

Pluralisation

Fill the gaps in these sentences with a plural noun.

1 Three blind m_____! Three blind m_____!

See how they run! See how they run!

2 All the c_____ walked into the hall very quietly.

3 I cut out the shape with a pair of
s_____.

4 I brush my t_____ every
morning and before I go to bed.

5 I can't go swimming because I have
lost my t_____.

6 My f_____ got wet because
I walked through all the puddles.

7 There are different toilets for m_____
and w_____.

8 One of the f_____ in our tank died today.

9 There were lots of s_____ in the field.

10 Ducks quack and g_____ honk.

Pluralisation

Rewrite these sentences in the plural.

1 A big lorry is coming slowly up the hill.

Two big _____

2 I had a sandwich for my lunch today.

I had two _____

3 I saw a monkey at the zoo. It was jumping around.

I saw two _____

4 I read a story before I went to bed last night.

I read two _____

5 I saw a fox in our garden last night. It was sniffing the dustbin.

I saw two _____

6 Today my class is going to the park.

Today all the _____

7 A workman came to fix the drains outside our house.

Two _____

8 You have to roll a six to start.

You have to roll two _____

9 A mouse ran quickly back into its hole.

Two _____

10 Matt put on his warm hat and woolly trousers and ran outside. He made deep marks in the snow by dragging his feet.

Matt and Kara_____

_____

Reading instructions

Follow these instructions to draw a clown's head.

1   Take a sheet of paper.

2   Draw a large circle in the middle of the sheet.

3   Draw a round nose in the middle of the circle.

4   Draw two big ears.

5   Draw a smiley mouth.

6   Draw two eyes.

7   Give your clown a pointed hat.

8   Draw three stripes on the hat.

9   Draw three bobbles on the side of the hat.

10 Give your clown a spotty bow-tie.

Share your pictures.
Can you see any differences?

Reading instructions

Follow these instructions carefully to draw a pattern.

1 Take a sheet of paper.

2 Draw a straight line across the middle of the sheet from left to right.

3 In the middle of the top half, draw a large circle.

4 Draw a smaller circle in the middle of this circle.

5 In the middle of the bottom half, draw a large square.

6 Divide the square in half by drawing a straight line from the top left-hand corner to the bottom right-hand corner.

7 On each side of the square, draw a small circle.

8 On each side of the large circle, draw a small triangle.

What have you got?

Compare your pattern with other people's.

Traditional stories

Draw lines to link the character with the adjective that describes him or her.

princess

giant

prince

step-mother

dragon

wolf

fairy godmother

witch

cunning

beautiful

wicked

hungry

kind

handsome

fierce

cruel

Choose one of the characters and write down the names of stories that he or she appears in.

_____

_____

_____

Traditional stories

Here are the beginnings and endings of three well-known stories.
Cut them out and match them up.
Then write down the titles of the stories.

Once upon a time there were three Bears who lived together in a house of their own, in a wood.

Once upon a time there was an old sow and she had three little pigs, and as she could not keep them she sent them to make their own way in the world.

And after that, the little Gingerbread Boy never said anything at all.

But the three Bears never saw anything more of her.

Once upon a time there was a little old woman and a little old man, and they lived all alone in a little old house.

And that was the end of the wolf.

Now cut out these sentences and match them to the right story.

"Run, run, as fast as you can."

"Then I'll huff and I'll puff and I'll blow your house down."

"Somebody has been sitting in my chair!"

Alphabetical texts and indexes

Imagine that you are the librarian in your school.
Fill in the chart to show where these new books should go.

title/author	fiction/ non-fiction	letter/ subject
Tusk, Tusk, David McKee		
Lucy's Day Trip, Jennifer Northway		
A Balloon for Grandad, Nigel Gray		
Tortoise's Dream, Joanna Troughton		
How the Animals Got their Colours, Michael Rosen		
A New Coat for Anna, Harriet Ziefert		
Food Around the World, J Ridgwell		
Stick Insects, Barrie Watts		
How Green Are You?, David Bellamy		
Two Victorian Families, Sue Wagstaff		
My Body, Your Body, Mick Manning		
Bridges, A and S MacGregor		
About the Weather, Barbara Taylor		

Alphabetical texts and indexes

These are the words for the index in a book about musical instruments.
Add three more of your own.
Then cut them out and sort them into alphabetical order.

tambourine	xylophone	cello
castanets	guitar	saxophone
flute	clarinet	organ
banjo	oboe	horn
drums	double bass	recorder
bassoon	harmonica	bells

Book reviews

Use this sheet to make notes about a book review you have read.

title of book _____

author _____

Tick the boxes to show what the reviewer writes about.

plot	☐	ideas in the book	☐
characters in the story	☐	the setting for the story	☐
style	☐	illustrations	☐
other books by this author	☐	who would like this book	☐
anything else?	☐		

What are the three main points that the reviewer makes about the book?
Note them down.

1 _____

_____

2 _____

_____

3 _____

_____

Book reviews

Use this sheet to plan a book review.
Make short notes under each heading.

title of book _____ author _____
introduction
plot
theme
setting
characters
style
conclusion

Characters

Choose from these words to fill the gaps in the sentences.

| asked | answered | replied | shouted | agreed | called |

| complained | exclaimed | mumbled |

1 "It's time you were in bed," _____ Mum.

"Oh, you never let me stay up," _____ Fran.
"It's not fair!"

2 "What's the opposite of 'rough'?" _____ the teacher.

"I know," _____ Yasmin. "It's smooth."

3 "Where are you going now?" _____ Elise.

"Not telling!" _____ Rachel. "It's none of your business."

4 "I've won!" _____ Kirby.

5 "It's not my fault," _____ Leanne.

"Speak up. I can't hear you," _____ her father.

6 "I really like playing this game," _____ Bridie.

"Yes, so do I," _____ Lacey. "It's fun."

Characters

Imagine this situation.

Three children – Jodie, Kara and Travis – are arguing about whose turn it is to take the hamster home for the weekend.

Write a conversation between them.

Use some of these words to describe the different ways they say things.

| say | complain | grumble | explain | snap | sigh | mutter |

| claim | agree | repeat | ask | reply | promise |

Dictionaries

The parts of these definitions have got muddled up!
Cut them out. Sort them out. Then stick them down to make two definitions.

Don't walk on thin ice.

thinner, thinnest

The cat had not eaten for many days and was very thin.

thin

He was terrified by the sound of thunder.

terrified, terrifies

verb

2 measuring a short distance from side to side

terrify

adjective

1 having little fat

to make someone very scared

Dictionaries

Find the word that fits both gaps in each pair of sentences.

1 I am going to join the swimming _____.

The giant carried a big _____.

2 I would like to live in a _____, high above the ground.

You can see a long way when the ground is _____.

3 My mum says that it is rude to _____.

You can't write neatly unless your pencil has a sharp

_____.

4 The pianist played a wrong _____.

I wrote a thank-you _____ to my gran.

5 I don't like having my finger- _____cut.

I fixed the shelf by banging in three _____.

Write more pairs of sentences like this for these words:

chip _____

_____

side _____

_____

Extended story

Use this sheet to plan your adventure story.

---

1 Two children become separated from adults.

Who are the adults? How do they get separated?

---

2 The children go to a new place.

What is the new place? How do they get there?

---

3 The children get into a mysterious or dangerous situation.

What happens? What is the danger or mystery? Do they meet someone? Do they get trapped? Or lost?

---

4 This situation is sorted out. The children and adults get back together.

Extended story

Use this sheet to make notes about yourself as an author.

place of birth _____

_____

age _____

_____

family _____

_____

_____

where you live _____

_____

interests and hobbies _____

_____

_____

where ideas for stories come from _____

_____

_____

First and third person narratives

Tick a box to show whether these stories are told in the first or third person.

	first person	third person

I woke up when the bomb came through the roof. It came through at an angle, overflew my bed by inches, bounced up over my mother's bed, hit the mirror, dropped into the grate and exploded up the chimney.

Jack's father and mother were dead, and the uncle and aunt were not very nice to him. What Jack didn't at all like was when the uncle and aunt took him for nice long walks in the fields instead of letting him go out alone with the dog.

My little brother Huey, my best friend Gloria and I were sitting on our front steps. It was one of those hot summer days when everything stands still. We didn't know what to do. We were watching the grass grow. It didn't grow fast.

Everybody knows the story of *The Three little Pigs* – or at least they think they do. But I'll let you in on a little secret. Nobody knows the real story, because nobody has ever heard my side of the story. I'm the wolf. Alexander T. Wolf.

It is early in the morning. In his warm and cosy bed, sunk in a soundproof slumber, Piper Paws dreams of chasing mice in a pastry shop. His alarm clock has not gone off, because late last night Piper took it apart. He wanted to find out what seconds, minutes and hours looked like.

When the sun goes down and the moon comes up and the old swing creaks in the dark, that's when we go to the park, me and Loopy and little Gee, all three. Softly down the staircase, through the haunty hall, trying to look small, me and Loopy and Little Gee, we three.

First and third person narratives

Fill the gaps in this story by adding the right pronoun.

"Mr Rabbit," said the little girl, "I want help."

"Help, little girl? I'll give you help if I can," said Mr Rabbit.

"Mr Rabbit," said the little girl, "it's about my mother."

"_____ mother?" said Mr Rabbit.

"It's _____ birthday," said the little girl.

"Happy birthday to _____ then," said Mr Rabbit. "What are _____ giving _____?"

"That's just it," said the little girl. "That's why ___ want help. ___ have nothing to give _____."

"Nothing to give _____ mother on _____ birthday?" said Mr Rabbit. "Little girl, _____ really do want help."

"___ would like to give _____ something that _____ likes," said the little girl.

"Something that _____ likes is a good present," said Mr Rabbit.

"But what?" said the little girl.

"Yes, what?" said Mr Rabbit.

"_____ likes red," said the little girl.

"Red," said Mr Rabbit. "_____ can't give _____ red."

"Something red, maybe," said the little girl.

"Oh, something red," said Mr Rabbit.

"What is red?" said the little girl.

"Well," said Mr Rabbit, "there's red underwear."

"No," said the little girl, "I can't give _____ that."

from *Mr Rabbit and the Lovely Present* by Charlotte Zolotow

Humorous poetry and language play

A pin has a head, but has no hair;
A clock has a face, but no mouth there;
Needles have eyes, but cannot see.

Finish these new lines for the poem.

A bottle has a neck, but _____

A clock has hands, but _____

A table has legs, but _____

A chair has arms, but _____

A mouth has a roof, but _____

A river has a mouth, but _____

Your fingers have nails, but _____

Humorous poetry and language play

The cheetah, my dearest,
is known not to cheat;
the tiger possesses no tie;
the horse-fly, of course,
was never a horse;
the lion will not tell a lie.

George Barker

Write new lines for this poem using these animals.

caterpillar _____

_____

penguin _____

_____

butterfly _____

_____

dragonfly _____

_____

starling _____

_____

seahorse _____

_____

badger _____

_____

dormouse _____

_____

hamster _____

_____

hedgehog _____

_____

Letters

Use this sheet to make notes about a letter you have read.

Who is it from? _____

Who is it to? _____

How does it begin? _____

For what purpose was it written? _____

_____

What are the main points?

- _____

- _____

- _____

- _____

How does it end? _____

_____

What else do you notice about how it is written?

_____

_____

_____

_____

_____

Letters

Draw lines to join the pronouns to the correct verbs.

Then finish the sentence.

I   is   _____

He   are   _____

They   am   _____

I   were   _____

We   was   _____

She   goes   _____

We   go   _____

I   plays   _____

He   play   _____

Poetry that uses sound

Write 'sound' words to go with these pictures.

_____

Poetry that uses sound

Complete the poem by adding rhyming words.

Fashion

I dye my hair bright green,

Unless I shave it _____.

I wear a wig upon my nose,

And bright earrings on my _____.

And though I know my legs are pylons,

I wear such pretty nylons.

Every day upon my shirt,

I dab a little grease and _____.

Brian Patten

Add rhyming words to these lists.

green	nose	shirt
_____	_____	_____
_____	_____	_____
_____	_____	_____
_____	_____	_____
_____	_____	_____
_____	_____	_____

Author study

Use this sheet to make notes about an author.

author's name _____

titles of four books by this author

1 _____

2 _____

3 _____

4 _____

facts about the author's life and work

_____

_____

_____

_____

_____

what's special about this author's books

_____

_____

_____

_____

_____

Author study

Choose from these 'time words' to fill the gaps in the story.
You will need to use some of the words more than once.

last		when		then		first		tomorrow		next		until

Winter had come and Anna needed a new coat. The fuzzy blue coat that she
had worn for so many winters was no longer fuzzy and it was very small.

"_____ winter" Anna's mother had said, "_____ the war is over, we will be
able to buy things again and I will get you a nice new coat."

But _____ the war ended the stores remained empty. There still were no
coats. There was hardly any food. And no one had any money.

Anna's mother wondered how she could get Anna a new coat. _____ she had
an idea. "Anna, I have no money," she said, "but I still have Grandfather's gold
watch and some other nice things. Maybe we can use them to get what we need
for a new coat. _____ we need wool. _____ we will visit a farmer and
see about getting some."

The _____ day Anna and her mother walked to a nearby farm.

"Anna needs a new coat," Anna's mother told the farmer. "I have no money, but
I will give you this fine gold watch if you will give me enough wool from your
sheep to make a coat."

The farmer said, "What a good idea! But you will have to wait _____ spring
_____ I shear my sheep's winter wool. _____ I can trade you their wool for
your gold watch …"

_____ spring came the farmer sheared the
sheep's wool.

"Does it hurt them?" asked Anna.

"No, Anna," said the farmer. "It is just like getting
a haircut."

_____ he had enough wool to make a coat, the farmer showed Anna how
to card the wool. "It's like untangling the knots in your hair," he told Anna.

_____ he gave Anna's mother a big bag of wool and Anna's mother gave
him the gold watch.

from *A New Coat for Anna* by Harriet Ziefert

Dialogue

In literacy work this week the children have been learning to read and write dialogue in stories.

The sentence-level focus has been on punctuation. Children have used full stops, question marks and exclamation marks at the end of sentences. They have begun to use speech marks to punctuate dialogue.

The word-level focus has been on using a range of words to introduce dialogue – not just 'said'.

In Anthony Browne's story *Knock Knock Who's There?* a little girl's father dresses up and pretends to frighten her.

Here is one episode from the story.

Rewrite it as a dialogue using speech bubbles or speech marks.

Add punctuation marks at the end of each sentence.

KNOCK KNOCK

Who's there

I'm a very creepy GHOST with a face as white as a sheet and chains that jangle and clank

When you let me in, I'm going to SPOOK you

Then I WON'T let you in

Who else could the girl's father dress up as?

Choose another scary character and write a new episode – just like the one in the book.

Fiction and non-fiction

In literacy work this week the children have been investigating the differences between fiction and non-fiction. They have read and written examples of both kinds of text.
The sentence-level focus has been on different ways of presenting texts.
The word-level focus has been on strategies for working out the meaning of new words.

Tick the right box to say whether these texts are fiction or non-fiction. Write another sentence for each.

fiction   **non-fiction**

Aa   Amy's apple
Bb   Bella's balloon
Cc   Carl's crayon

☐   ☐

_____

_____

Long ago there were no colours in the world at all. Almost everything was grey, and what was not grey was black or white. It was a time called The Great Greyness.
    Every morning a Wizard who lived during the time of The Great Greyness would open his window to look out at the wide land. _____

☐   ☐

_____

_____

One winter morning Peter woke up and looked out of the window. Snow had fallen during the night. It covered everything as far as he could see.
    After breakfast he put on his snowsuit and ran outside. _____

☐   ☐

_____

_____

Elephants have very large ears. They flap them to keep flies away. _____

☐   ☐

_____

_____

Non-chronological reports

In literacy work this week the children have been finding out about how information is organised in non-chronological reports.

The sentence-level focus has been on writing in sentences and punctuating them with capital letters and full stops.

The word-level focus has been on words beginning with prefixes.

Write a word beginning with these prefixes.

re_____   ex_____   dis_____

un_____   mis_____   pre_____

Write about your class under these headings and sub-headings.

LESSONS

_____

_____

_____

Music

_____

_____

_____

PE

_____

_____

_____

Organisation and presentation of information

In literacy work this week the children have been investigating the different ways in which information is presented and organised in non-fiction books. They have been learning to use contents lists, indexes and glossaries.
The word-level focus has been on working out the meaning of new words.

Write down the name of a subject you are interested in and know a lot about.

_____

Think of three special words to do with the subject.
Write them down in alphabetical order.
Write glossary entries to explain what they mean.

1 _____ ---------------------------------

----

2 _____ ---------------------------------

----

3 _____ ---------------------------------

Playscripts

In literacy work this week the children have been reading and writing playscripts. The sentence-level focus has been on punctuating sentences with full stops, question marks and exclamation marks.

Rewrite this strip cartoon as a playscript.

Jack and the Beanstalk

_____

_____

_____

_____

_____

_____

_____

Poems of observation and the senses

> In literacy work this week the children have been reading, comparing and writing poems.
> The sentence-level focus has been on verbs that describe action vividly.
> The word-level focus has been on rhyming words and synonyms.

Find the patterns and rhymes in this poem.

Anna Elise, she jumped with surprise;
The surprise was so quick, it played her a trick;
The trick was so rare, she jumped in a chair;
The chair was so frail, she jumped in a pail;
The pail was so set, she jumped in a net;
The net was so small, she jumped on the ball;
The ball was so round, she jumped on the ground;
And ever since then she's been turning around.

Anon

Try writing a new ending for each of the six lines in the middle of the poem.

The surprise was so quick, _____

The trick was so rare, _____

The chair was so frail, _____

The pail was so set, _____

The net was so small, _____

The ball was so round. _____

Try writing some new lines with the same pattern as these.

_____

_____

_____

Settings

In literacy work this week the children have been exploring how settings are described in stories. They have written their own descriptions of places. The word-level focus has been on strategies for spelling new words and on collecting and choosing between synonyms.

This is the beginning of Raymond Briggs' version of *Jack and the Beanstalk*.

Early one morning Jim woke up and saw an <u>enormous</u> plant growing outside his window.

"That's <u>funny</u>," he <u>said</u>, "it wasn't there yesterday. I'll see how high it goes," and he <u>began</u> to climb up the plant.

"It certainly is a <u>big</u> plant," he said, as he <u>went into</u> the clouds.

When he <u>reached</u> the top of the plant, Jim saw a castle.

"I'm hungry," he said. "I'll ask at the castle for breakfast. I hope they have cornflakes."

Jim <u>ran</u> to the castle and knocked on the door. He waited and waited, until the door was slowly opened by a very old giant.

from *Jim and the Beanstalk*, Raymond Briggs

Look at the underlined words.
Write two words that the author might have used instead.

enormous	_____	_____
funny	_____	_____
said	_____	_____
began	_____	_____
big	_____	_____
went into	_____	_____
reached	_____	_____
ran	_____	_____

Shape poems

In literacy work this week the children have been looking at, reading and writing different kinds of shape poems and calligrams (poems in which the style of the letters suggests the meaning).

The sentence-level focus has been on verbs that describe action vividly.

The word-level focus has been on spelling verbs ending in *ing* and on synonyms for the word 'say'.

Write one-word shape poems using these verbs that describe different ways of moving.

Make the style and arrangement of the letters fit the meaning.

skip

slide

wriggle

dance

Choose other verbs like this, and make more poems!

Thesauruses

In literacy work this week the focus has been on words. The children have been learning how to use thesauruses to find words with similar meanings. They have chosen interesting and precise words for their writing and practised strategies for spelling new words.

Solve this word puzzle by finding synonyms for the words in the clues.

1 turn	T
2 difficult	H
3 like	E
4 slide	S
5 quarrel	A
6 strange	U
7 mend	R
8 sad	U
9 tiny	S

Verbs

In literacy work this week the children have been learning about verbs.
The sentence-level focus has been on changing the tense of verbs.
The word-level focus has been on spelling patterns for verbs and on extending vocabulary.

Write two sentences about what you did in school today. Start like this.

In school today I _____

_____

In school today we _____

_____

Write two sentences about what you are doing right now. Start like this.

Right now I am _____

_____

Right now I am _____

_____

Write two sentences about what you are going to do when you have finished this homework. Start like this.

When I have finished this homework, I am _____

_____

When I have finished this homework, I will _____

_____

Characters

In literacy work this week the children have been focusing on characters in stories. They have found out about how characters are shown through description and dialogue, and have written character portraits.

The sentence-level focus has been on adjectives and capital letters for names.
The word-level focus has been on words ending with suffixes and on using apostrophes in spelling shortened forms of words.

Choose someone you like – a friend or someone in your family. Draw and write about him or her.

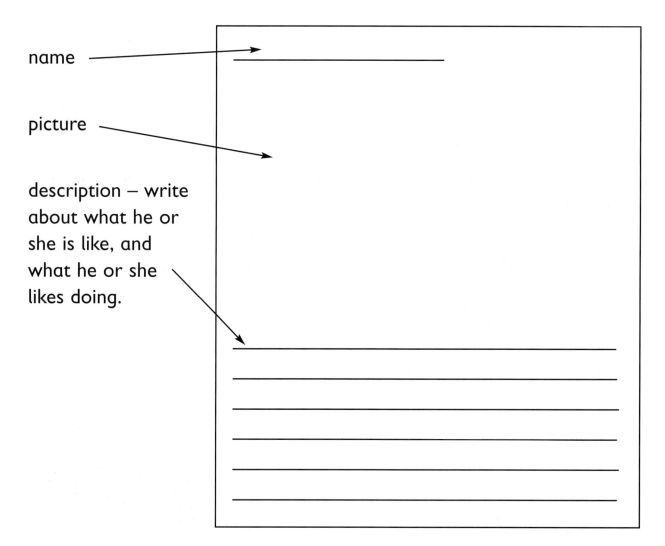

name

picture

description – write about what he or she is like, and what he or she likes doing.

Dictionaries

In literacy work this week the focus has been on word-level work. The children have learned more about finding words in dictionaries and using them to check spellings and the meanings of words. They have investigated silent letters and the spelling of words ending in suffixes.

Fill the gaps to write more sentences like this.

My handwriting is neat, but Sally's is **neater** and Bing's is the **neatest** of all.

1 My gloves are thick, but Saskia's are _____ and Chloe's are _____ of all.

2 I looked sad, but Travis looked _____ and Harley looked _____ of all.

3 My bedroom is messy, but my sister's is _____ and my big brother's is _____ of all.

Add *ly* to these words and use them to fill the gaps in these sentences.

| quick | | gentle | | noisy |

1 Our cat likes to be tickled _____ under the chin.

2 Mrs Ross told us to stop playing so _____.

3 I ran so _____ that I wasn't late for school.

PURR!

Fables

> In literacy work this week the children have been reading and writing fables. They have investigated animal characters in these stories and the morals that they illustrate.
> The sentence-level focus has been on adjectives.
> The word-level focus has been on opposites and on words ending with suffixes.

Read this fable.

A lion found a hare fast asleep by the road. He was just about to eat it when he saw a deer running by. He left the hare alone and ran off after the deer. The hare woke up and ran away.

The lion chased the deer for a long time but the deer was too quick for him. The lion realised that he would never catch up.

So the lion went back to where the hare had been sleeping by the road. But the hare was nowhere to be seen.

"It serves me right," said the lion, "for leaving the food I had in the hope of catching something bigger."

Give the fable a title and a moral.

TITLE _____

MORAL _____

Write words that have an opposite meaning to these words from the story.

quick   _____   asleep   _____

long   _____   never   _____

up   _____   back   _____

nowhere _____   right   _____

bigger   _____   found   _____

Making notes

In literacy work this week the children have been making clear, short notes in different ways and for different purposes. They have used lists and charts to do this. The sentence-level focus has been on deleting words that are not essential to the main idea.

Imagine that Red Riding Hood realises that the Wolf has taken her Grandmother's place in the bed. She runs out of the house, and locks the door behind her.

Write a telegram message from Red Riding Hood to her mother, explaining the situation and asking for help.

Words cost 10p each and you have £1.00.

Use this chart to make notes about the advantages and disadvantages of being an only child.

advantages	disadvantages

Myths and legends

In literacy work this week the children have been reading myths about how animals acquired their different characteristics. They have written their own myth.
The sentence-level focus has been on adjectives and on writing in brief notes.
The word-level focus has been on new words and on changing nouns into adjectives by adding the letter *y*.

This is the beginning of the story of how the turtle got its shell. Which words can you cross out but still keep the main ideas?

Once upon a time, Turtle did not have a shell to cover her back. This is the story of how she got it.

One fine, sunny day, Turtle came clambering slowly out of the sea and up onto the warm, sandy beach. She wandered around, here and there, until she found a beautiful garden. Inside this beautiful garden there stood a tall, tall tree hung from top to bottom with huge yellow bananas.

Choose one of these animals.

the giraffe – and its neck

the elephant – and its trunk

Write a very short story explaining how it got this part of its body.

_____

_____

_____

_____

Performance poetry

In literacy work this week the children have been reading, rehearsing and performing poems.
The sentence-level focus has been on commas.
The word-level focus has been on counting syllables and spelling words with long vowel sounds.

Count the syllables in these words.

carrots ☐   celery ☐

cabbage ☐   grapes ☐

lollipops ☐   watermelon ☐

Write other food words with:

one syllable _____ _____ _____
two syllables _____ _____ _____
three syllables _____ _____ _____

Count the syllables in the lines of this poem.

What starts the thunder overhead? ☐

Who makes the crashing noise? ☐

Are the angels falling out of bed? ☐

Are they breaking all their toys? ☐

Why does the sun go down so soon? ☐

Why do the night-clouds crawl ☐

Hungrily up to the new-laid moon ☐

And swallow it, shell and all? ☐

from *Questions at Night* by Louis Untermeyer

What do you notice? _____

143

Pluralisation

In literacy work this week the focus has been on sentence- and word-level work. Children have developed their understanding of the meaning of 'singular' and 'plural' and how to make sure they use the correct grammatical forms of verbs. They have investigated spelling rules for adding s to change nouns from singular to plural.

Fill in the gaps with a plural noun.
Remember the spelling rules for adding _s_!

one bus   two _____ in a row

one class   both Year 3 _____

a peach   a bowl of _____

an ostrich   two _____

a box of crayons   three _____ of crayons

one buzz   two _____

a match   a box of _____

a fly   lots of _____

a dish   all the _____

one family   three _____

Remember these are unusual plurals!

one mouse   a family of _____

one child   lots of _____

one pair of trousers   two pairs of _____

one foot   both _____

one sheep   a flock of _____

one man and one woman   two _____ and two _____

Reading instructions

In literacy work this week the children have been reading and following instructions. They have learned about the style of instructions and how they are organised and presented.

The sentence-level focus has been on using commas in lists.

The word-level focus has been on opposites.

Put commas between the items in these lists.

When I go swimming I always take my goggles a big fluffy towel my swimming hat and 50p for the locker.

My favourite breakfast is a bowl of cereal a piece of toast jam and a cup of tea.

We made a model windmill out of cardboard a cork string two wooden rods and strong glue.

Complete these pairs of opposites.

beautiful	_____	follow	_____
sharp	_____	more	_____
worst	_____	together	_____
all	_____	bigger	_____
before	_____	happy	_____
full	_____	heavy	_____
odd	_____	begin	_____
win	_____	straight	_____

Write some more pairs of opposites.

_____   _____

_____   _____

_____   _____

Traditional stories

In literacy work this week the children have been exploring the characters, themes and language of traditional tales.
The sentence-level focus has been on adjectives and adverbs.
The word-level focus has been on words ending with suffixes.

Use this chart to make notes about your favourite traditional tale.

title _____ setting or settings
main character
other characters
theme
main events •   •   •   •

Writing instructions

In literacy work this week the children have been writing different kinds of instruction. They have learned about the style of instructions and how they are organised and presented.

The sentence-level focus has been on using commas in lists.

The word-level focus has been on spelling rules for changing nouns from singular to plural.

Edit this recipe by adding commas to the lists and correcting the mistakes with plural nouns.

Banana milkshakes for two peoples

You will need:

a large banana 2 teaspoonses of sugar a cupful of milk

a knife a chopping board 2 glassis to serve the milkshakes in

a blender

1 Chop the banana into small sliceses.
2 Put the chopped banana into the blender.
3 Add the milk and sugar.
4 Turn the blender on for one minute.
5 Turn the blender off.
6 Pour the milkshake into two glass.

Write instructions:

to make your teacher smile

_____

_____

to make a cat purr

_____

_____

Alphabetical texts and indexes

In literacy work this week the children have been learning about the classification of books in libraries, and how to locate information in alphabetically organised materials quickly and efficiently. They have written their own encyclopedia entries for a subject they are interested in.

The word-level focus has been on developing spelling strategies by identifying similarities between words.

floppy   Write down 3 words.

in the same 'family'   _____   _____   _____

beginning with *fl*   _____   _____   _____

ending with *y*   _____   _____   _____

with double *p*   _____   _____   _____

Choose something that you are interested in.
Choose two important words to do with this subject.
Write encyclopedia entries for these words.

Book reviews

In literacy work this week the children have been reading and writing book reviews, and have written a letter to an author. They have also made notes and summarised the main points in stories and reviews. The sentence-level focus has been on commas and linking sentences clearly.

On another sheet of paper write a short review of a book, television programme or film that you have read or seen recently.

Write two sentences about what you liked, and one sentence about what you did not like so much.

Read the first sentence in each pair. Then finish the second sentence.
Re-read both sentences to make sure that they fit together and make sense.

1 We are going to have a barbecue on the beach tonight. If _____

_____

2 It took a long time to get the car fixed. While _____

_____

3 Last week I nearly had a bad accident on my skateboard. Since ___

_____

4 We looked everywhere for my little brother's teddy bear but we couldn't find it. So _____

_____

Characters

In literacy work this week the children have been investigating characters in fiction. They have talked about how different characters feel and behave, and learned about how authors describe characters.

The sentence-level focus has been on pronouns, and on punctuating and setting out dialogue.

The word-level focus has been on using apostrophes to spell shortened forms of words, and on using different words for describing how people talk.

Who is your favourite character in fiction? _____

What do you like about this character? _____

_____

_____

Write a list of words to describe what this character looks like and how she or he behaves. _____

_____

_____

Imagine you met this character.
What would you say to him or her? _____

_____

_____

How would he or she reply? _____

_____

_____

Dictionaries

In literacy work this week the children have been learning to use dictionaries quickly and efficiently. They have also been writing their own dictionary entries. The word-level focus has been on: the different kinds of information that dictionaries provide; homonyms (words with more than meaning); and words beginning with prefixes.

Choose a word that you especially like, maybe because of the way it sounds or what it reminds you of.

Write a dictionary entry for this word.

word ⟶ _____   _____ ⟵ word class

definition
⟶ _____

_____

use the ⟶ _____
word in a
sentence _____

_____ _____ _____ ⟵ words in the same family

_____

What sort of pen is a flightless sea bird? _____

What sort of pill do you lay your head on? _____

What kind of pin is a colour? _____

What kind of pet grows on a flower? _____

What kind of pan can you eat? _____

Write your own questions like this.

151

Extended story

In literacy work this week the children have been planning and writing a long adventure story organised in chapters. They have developed the characters and the setting for this story, and have worked on creating suspense and excitement. The sentence-level focus has been on punctuating dialogue and using words that show the passing of time.

How does Reuben get out of this dangerous situation? Write what happens next in this adventure story.

Reuben had climbed nearly to the top of the tree when he heard a loud cracking noise. The branch he was standing on had broken! Before he knew what was happening, he was slipping and then he was falling. He grabbed at branches but couldn't hold on. Then suddenly, with a jolt, he stopped falling. The baggy jumper he was wearing had caught on a branch, and he was hanging in the air. He looked down and realised that he was still a long way above the ground.

_____

_____

_____

_____

_____

Imagine that a friend of yours is an author. Draw a picture of their face, and write their author profile. Include information about their age, where they live, their family and their interests and hobbies.

_____

_____

_____

_____

_____

First and third person narratives

In literacy work this week the children have been learning how to tell the difference between stories in the first person and the third person. They have written stories in both ways.
The sentence-level focus has been on pronouns, and on making sure that pronouns and verbs 'agree'.
The word-level focus has been on using apostrophes to spell shortened forms of words.

Choose the right pronouns to fill the gaps in this story.

The Wizard would often go down the stairs to _____ dark, grey cellar. There, just to amuse _____, and to forget about the drab world outside, _____ would make wonderful magic potions and spells.

One day, while the Wizard was mixing and stirring a little of this and a little of that, _____ saw something strange in the bottom of _____ pot.

"What good-looking stuff _____ have made!" _____ exclaimed. "_____ will make some right away."

"What is _____?" asked the neighbours, when _____ saw the Wizard painting _____ house.

"A colour," cried the neighbours. "_____ calls _____ blue."

"Please," cried the neighbours, "please give _____ some!"

"Of course," said the Wizard.

from *The Great Blueness and Other Predicaments* by Arnold Lobel

Humorous poetry and language play

In literacy work this week the children have been reading different kinds of humorous poetry and word play, including nonsense verse, cautionary tales, acrostics and puns.

The word-level focus has been on investigating homonyms (words with more than one meaning) and their use in jokes.

Write sentences showing two different meanings of these words.

fair

1 _____

2 _____

band

1 _____

2 _____

nail

1 _____

2 _____

Fill the gaps in this nonsense poem.

As I was going out one day
My head _____ _____ and rolled _____
But when I saw that it was gone,
I _____ it up and put it on.

And when I got into the street
A fellow cried: "Look at your _____!"
I looked at them and sadly said:
"I've left them both _____ in _____!"

Letters

In literacy work this week the children have been reading and writing different kinds of letter. They have learned about how letters are set out and the different ways they can begin and end.

The sentence-level focus has been on pronouns, and on making sure that pronouns and verbs 'agree'.

The word-level focus has been on different common expressions, e.g. for saying thank you or apologising.

Fill the gaps in this conversation with the right pronoun. Read it through to make sure it makes sense.

"I can't find _____ hat. Do _____ know where _____ is?"

"No, _____ don't. Hats don't move. I expect it's just where _____ left _____. Have you looked under _____ bed?"

"Yes, _____ have. _____ is not there. And I've looked in _____ toy-box, too, and _____ is not there either."

"Well, have _____ looked in _____ sister's room? Maybe it got mixed up with _____ clothes."

Read this letter.

Dear Zak,

I am really glad that you can come to my Hallowe'en Party next week.

I am asking everyone to dress up as a ghost or a witch. Please write and tell me what you will dress up as.

I would also like everyone to learn a trick to show the others. If you need anything for your trick, let me know.

See you on Sunday.

Miranda

On another sheet of paper write Zak's reply to Miranda.

Poetry that uses sound

In literacy work this week the children have been learning how the sound of words is used in poetry. They have investigated alliteration, rhyme and rhythm.
The word-level focus has been on revising different ways of spelling vowel and consonant phonemes.

Write a word that begins with the same sound but a different letter.

kick _____   foot _____

seat _____   rat _____

net _____   cat _____

Practise reading this poem out loud.
Try to get the rhythm and sounds just right.

New shoes, new shoes,
Red and pink and blue shoes,
Tell me what would you choose
If they'd let you buy?

Buckle shoes, bow shoes,
Pretty pointy-toe shoes,
Strappy, cappy low shoes;
Let's have some to try.

Bright shoes, white shoes,
Dandy dance-by-night shoes,
Perhaps-a-little-tight shoes;
Like some? So would I.

BUT

Flat shoes, fat shoes,
Stump-along-like-that shoes,
Wipe-them-on-the-mat shoes,
O that's the sort they'll buy.

Ffrida Wolfe

Author study

In literacy work this week the children have been investigating the work of particular authors. They have identified what makes it special, and how it changes from book to book. They have also written book reviews.
The sentence-level focus has been on using words that show the passing of time.
The word-level focus has been on collecting new words and learning how to spell them.

Use this sheet to make notes about your favourite author.

My favourite author is _____

Four books written by this author:

1 _____

2 _____

3 _____

4 _____

Three things I like about this author's books:

1 _____

I like this because _____

2 _____

I like this because _____

3 _____

I like this because _____

My favourite book by this author is _____

I like this book best because _____

Notes

Notes